E.T.™

THE *EXTRA-TERRESTRIAL*
FROM CONCEPT TO CLASSIC

The Illustrated Story of the
Film and the Filmmakers

Introduction by STEVEN SPIELBERG
Screenplay by MELISSA MATHISON
Interviews by LAURENT BOUZEREAU
Edited by LINDA SUNSHINE
Designed by TIMOTHY SHANER

A NEWMARKET PICTORIAL MOVIEBOOK

NEWMARKET PRESS · NEW YORK

Library of Congress Cataloging-in-Publication Data available upon request.

ISBN 1-55704-560-7 Gift Set Edition
ISBN 1-55704-513-5 (Newmarket trade paperback edition)
ISBN 1-55704-504-6 (Newmarket trade hardcover edition)

www.newmarketpress.com

Design by Timothy Shaner

Manufactured in the United States of America

Other Newmarket Pictorial Moviebooks include:
Ali: The Movie and the Man
Planet of the Apes: Re-imagined by Tim Burton
Moulin Rouge: The Splendid Book That Charts the Journey of Baz Luhrmann's Motion Picture
The Art of The Matrix
Gladiator: The Making of the Ridley Scott Epic
Crouching Tiger, Hidden Dragon: A Portrait of the Ang Lee Film
Titus: The Illustrated Screenplay, Adapted from the Play by William Shakespeare
The Age of Innocence: A Portrait of the Film Based on the Novel by Edith Wharton
Cradle Will Rock: The Movie and the Moment
The Sense and Sensibility Screenplay and Diaries
Saving Private Ryan: The Men, the Mission, the Movie
Amistad: A Celebration of the Film by Steven Spielberg
Bram Stoker's Dracula: The Film and the Legend

Contents

Introduction

Bringing Back the Magic

When production started on *E.T.* more than twenty years ago, none of us could have dreamed there would be a twentieth anniversary release and a book such as this. We had no illusions about the ultimate success of the film, but we knew it was a story we wanted to tell and we told it the way we wanted to tell it.

You will get a real sense of that as you go through this journey with me and those who joined in bringing E.T. and *E.T.* to life. We want to invite you into our filmmaking family and take you behind the scenes—behind the magic, surprises, and emotional experiences that meant so much in our own lives. This book is our *E.T.* family album filled with details from our personal memory banks and production archives.

For me, *E.T.* was—and still is—my most personal film.

The journey actually began when I was growing up in Scottsdale, California. Suburbia. They say write what you know, and it's the same with filmmaking.

In suburbia, you can look up at the clear night sky, and I've always been intrigued with outer space, starting as early as five years old. One night, my dad woke me up and took me out in a field, laid out a picnic blanket, and we stared at a fantastic meteor shower. I saw all those streaks of light moving across the sky, and it gave a jump-start to my fascination with the universe.

Science fiction was big then as it is now. Dad would read a lot of it—stories filled with scary aliens taking over the world—but he never imagined it that way. He would say he thought if other life forms had the technology to travel all those light years, they would never do it to spread hate and evil—they'd do it to satisfy their curiosity. They would want to share their knowledge with other planetary systems and other species. That's what I tried to show in both *Close Encounters of the Third Kind* and *E.T.*

ABOVE: Steven Spielberg poses for a publicity photo with his lead actor in E.T. LEFT: A still from the original 1982 release of the film.

There's a lot of my life in the film. All the kids are combinations of my family and me. I intended the film to reflect the feelings I had as a kid, although I wasn't very articulate about that when I talked to reporters at press junkets in 1982. I never once mentioned that the movie also grew out of the divorce of my parents, although it was always there subconsciously. Then it finally hit me and I felt comfortable including it.

The *E.T.* concept bounced around in my head for years. I came up with the original story and Melissa Mathison wrote a genius screenplay, which for the first time, is included here as the centerpiece for the book. You'll see how the ideas and words became dialogue and images that have become part of our collective culture.

The positive impact that *E.T.* had on audiences throughout the world was perhaps the most rewarding result of what became a phenomenon. Two examples drove that home. The first was a letter from Eunice Shriver of the Special Olympics. She recognized that our extraterrestrial, a creature who was different, represented the same spirit of overcoming challenges as demonstrated by the athletes of Special Olympics. The other was a note from a mother who said that her autistic child, who had not spoken, spoke his first words after seeing *E.T.* Something in that heart light reached out.

Would there ever be a sequel to *E.T.*? That's been the most-asked question, and I've had the same response for twenty years: "I'm not going to do it." A sequel would diffuse the memory of the first one. Instead, I thought it would be great to reissue the movie and the twentieth anniversary seemed the perfect opportunity to put it back in theaters where I most want people to see it. A generation has grown up since the film was last in theatres. Some of you reading this now may have seen it as a child and now have your own children—mothers and dads now have grandkids.

Everyone involved in making *E.T.* is thrilled to have this opportunity for a re-release. The film has always been a celebration of friendship and love and promoting understanding between races and cultures. As I said, I never imagined it could become such a phenomenon. I simply wanted to tell this story, which was so close to my heart.

I hope you will agree that E.T.'s heart light glows as well as ever.

—Steven Spielberg
January 2002

ABOVE: The moon, used in the scene of Elliott and E.T. flying, was shot in Nicasio, Calfornia, near the ILM studios. The image became the logo for Amblin Entertainment.

PART ONE:
FROM CONCEPT TO CASTING

The NIGHT SKIES of a BOY'S LIFE

In the Beginning There Was *Night Skies*

One of the things that really inspired me to work with Steven was *Close Encounters of the Third Kind*. The movie had a profound effect on me and, more than anything, was the catalyst that convinced me I wanted to make movies as a career. When I did, in fact, find myself eventually working with Steven, one of the things we discussed was the research he had done with a scientist and astronomer named J. Allen Hynek during the making of *Close Encounters*.

Steven asked me to investigate a particular case about a farm family that was terrorized one evening by gremlin-like, extraterrestrials. They supposedly surrounded the house, trying to get access. They also rode the cows through the barnyard and made the people crazy.
— KATHLEEN KENNEDY, PRODUCER

When I read an early draft about the farm family case [*Night Skies*], I didn't feel it was a movie I wanted to direct. It was too violent and went against my own beliefs that aliens would come to earth with bad intentions. Personally, I never thought that would be the case. I thought they would come here to either observe at a distance or to interact in some kind of healthy way.

It went against my grain as a filmmaker and story teller to tell an aggressive, scary story about aliens attacking a farm house. That's when everything changed in my mind and I realized I was not going to make that movie, but I might make another movie about an alien who gets left behind on earth, an idea that came from the ending of *Close Encounters* when the spaceship door closes.
— STEVEN SPIELBERG, DIRECTOR/PRODUCER

PREVIOUS PAGE: An original painting by Ed Verreaux of the landing of E.T.'s spaceship. ABOVE: Producer Kathleen Kennedy and director Steven Spielberg wearing hard hats during the filming of the movie. LEFT: Early concept for a poster of the 1982 release.

13

The Concept:
How *E.T.* Got Started

I'd always wanted to tell the story of a disenfranchised and lonely boy in a relationship with his siblings. I also wanted to tell a story about a young child's reaction to his parents' divorce and how that impacts him for the rest of his life. So the story was on my mind for maybe fifteen or twenty years. Also, it was a childhood fantasy of mine to tell the story of a special, best friend who rescues a young boy from the sadness of a divorce. So, *E.T.* came about in stages for me.

Sometime in 1979 or 1980, we were shooting *Raiders of the Lost Ark* in Tunisia and, during one of the long set ups, I was walking in the desert, picking up prehistoric sea shells, and trying to figure out how I could tell the story of this lonely boy. At the time I was feeling kind of separate from myself, which often happens when you are directing. You

go into a kind of fugue state to make a movie. So I was in one of these states of mind when, bang, this concept hit me and the story began to flood into my mind. For the next couple of days, during the shooting of *Raiders*, the bones of the story began to fall into place.

It took me two or three days to figure out the beginning, the middle, and the end of the story. Then I remembered loving this movie called *The Black Stallion* which had been co-authored by Melissa Mathison, who was on the set of *Raiders* with Harrison Ford.

I asked Melissa to write the script, but she was reluctant at first so I started nagging her about it. I went to Harrison and said, "Harrison, talk to Melissa, I think she should write this movie." Then Kathy Kennedy talked to Melissa. The two of them, Kathy and Harrison, convinced Melissa to at least do a first draft for me. And that's how it all got started.
—STEVEN SPIELBERG

ABOVE: Producer Kathleen Kennedy and director Steven Spielberg on the set during the filming of the school scene where Elliott releases the frogs in his science class.

Early Ideas

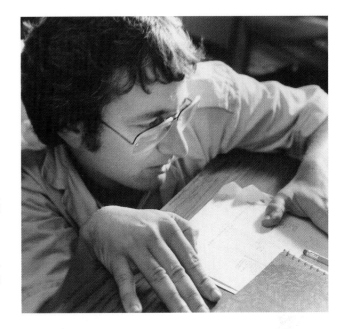

Many of the scenes from the movie come from my own experiences with children.

I would ask Willard and Benjamin, Harrison's sons, and their friends and other kids what kind of powers they would like from an alien. A lot of the children mentioned the obvious: telepathy or telekinetic powers. But I was struck by the fact that several of them said they would like this magic creature to be able to heal. I thought it was such an incredibly poignant idea to come from a child. They weren't talking about saving someone's life by healing. They were talking about taking the "owies" away. And of course, E.T. heals.

Very early on, Steven Spielberg and I decided that we didn't want to have any adults mucking up the works. This was important for a couple of reasons. First of all, E.T. is this little creature. The earth that he experiences is small and filled with little people his own size. When he returned to his planet, he would be reporting on a planet that was populated by children, which we thought was a poetic idea.

Secondly, Elliott had to have the power in the movie. If even for a moment an adult took away Elliott's power before it became a matter of life and death, then Elliott would have lost all of his magic.

—MELISSA MATHISON, SCREENWRITER/
ASSOCIATE PRODUCER

I never wanted to show grown-ups in the movie until the very end. I wanted to suggest them, like in a *Tom & Jerry* cartoon where, when the mom comes in, you only see her from the waist down. I was raised with television and with cartoons so this made sense to me. I didn't want that world contaminated with anything beyond a young teenager's point of view.

I was also very interested in the idea that E.T. could communicate psychically with Elliott. He could reach out to Elliott in school and give him ideas while he was sitting in class. If E.T. got drunk, for example, Elliott got drunk.

Elliott would start becoming and feeling E.T.'s psychic spirit inside of him. That was really interesting to me. I didn't know where those ideas were going to fall into the structure of the movie. But these were like my wish list. Can we put this in the movie? Can we put that in the movie?

—STEVEN SPIELBERG

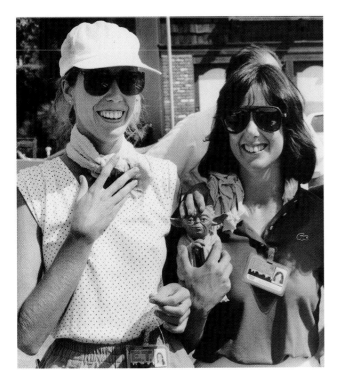

LEFT: *Writer Melissa Mathison and producer Kathleen Kennedy during the filming of the Halloween scenes.* ABOVE RIGHT: *Director Steven Spielberg setting up a shot in Elliott's classroom.*

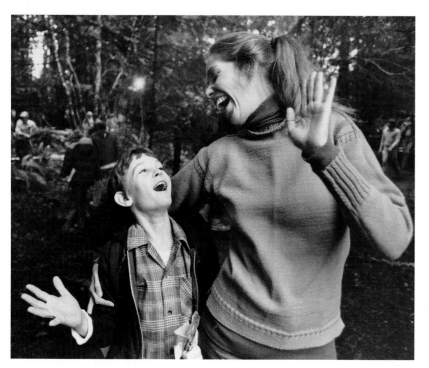

The Script: Writing the First Draft

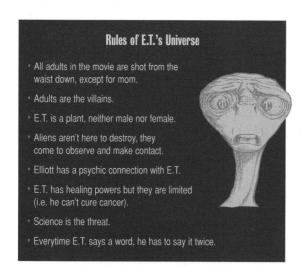

Rules of E.T.'s Universe

- All adults in the movie are shot from the waist down, except for mom.

- Adults are the villains.

- E.T. is a plant, neither male nor female.

- Aliens aren't here to destroy, they come to observe and make contact.

- Elliott has a psychic connection with E.T.

- E.T. has healing powers but they are limited (i.e. he can't cure cancer).

- Science is the threat.

- Everytime E.T. says a word, he has to say it twice.

As I remember it, I would write for four or five days in my little office in Hollywood, and then drive out to Marina Del Rey where Steven Spielberg was editing in a little apartment on the beach. I'd bring him my pages and we'd sit and go through them. We would decide what worked and what didn't and where we'd go from there. Then we would talk about the next hunk that should be written. I'd go back to my little office and do my writing and come back again a few days later to meet him.

It took eight weeks for us to get the first draft, which was quite fast, I think.

—MELISSA MATHISON

Melissa delivered this 107-page first draft to me and I read it in about an hour. I was just knocked out. It was a script I was willing to shoot the next day. It was so honest, and Melissa's voice made a direct connection with my heart.

—STEVEN SPIELBERG

I was having lunch with an executive at MGM. In fact, we were discussing *Poltergeist* which we were making at the time. Steven came running into the commissary with this screenplay and he said, "I've just read Melissa's first draft. We could shoot this tomorrow. It's the best first draft I've ever read." I think, in many respects, Steven would say that that's still true, even today.

—KATHLEEN KENNEDY

RIGHT: Producer Kathleen Kennedy poses with the star of the movie during the first release of the movie. ABOVE: Writer Melissa Mathison clowning around on the set with actor Henry Thomas.

CREATING the CREATURE

Shopping for a Designer

I went to several designers to find my single creature. I had one concept for E.T. that was pretty consistent with all the designers. I didn't want anybody to think that E.T. was anything other than an actual extraterrestrial. Therefore, it couldn't look like there was somebody in a suit. I wanted him to be only three feet tall. So, I needed him to have a small neck and I want the neck to telescope, like a turtle coming out of his shell. The neck defied the idea of a human being being inside that suit. That was a concept I came up with even back during *Close Encounters*.

Ed Verreaux did some sketching for me and we gave Carlo Rambaldi some of the sketches. Carlo had created one of the creatures in *Close Encounters of the Third Kind*. He designed Puck with a very tiny neck. I love Carlo's designs.

—STEVEN SPIELBERG

In the early stages, we didn't really know what E.T. was going to look like because we were just sort of talking about him. At some point, fairly early on, we set down some ground rules. First, that E.T. isn't a monster.

The thing I really remember very specifically working with Steven was going into his office and looking at all these books. He would say, those are neat eyes, that's a neat mouth. Look at this person. They were really interesting because they would be some very, very, very old people with these very old, wizened eyes.

Then Carlo and I would go away for a day or two and we would draw a lot of stuff. We would just basic shotgun. Then we would go back to Steven's office and pin the stuff up on the wall. Steven would look at them and tell us what he liked and didn't like.

—ED VERREAUX

LEFT: E.T. as photographed in the 1982 release of the movie.
ABOVE: Carlo Rambaldi pointing to the original sketches of the extraterrestrial.

I came to America about twenty-five years ago to work on the remake of *King Kong* for Dino De Laurentiis. When I was finished, I got a call from Steven Spielberg. He explained that he wasn't happy with the look of one of his aliens in *Close Encounters of the Third Kind*, and asked me to come up with some ideas. I ended up doing something that Steven liked, and a few years later, he called me to work on *E.T.* I did not do many sketches at first, but I did look at an abstract painting called *Women of Delta* that I had done for the Academy of Fine Arts in Italy, showing women with very long necks. And that was a departure for me. Steven then came to my shop many times, and we worked together. We had different types of E.T.s, different heads, and several ways to approach each scene, including using little people, a boy with no legs in a suit, and a mime for the arms and hands in some cases.

When we were working with the mechanical E.T., using levers, the cables were hidden underneath the floor, and I would be standing off-stage with several other puppeteers, watching E.T. on a video screen and trying to improve his great performance. It was challenging because it was difficult to see the image clearly on the video monitor, but we managed and I think Steven was happy.

During the shooting, everyone who worked with us showed a lot of respect for E.T. Everyone seemed to forget that he was not real, and they definitely treated him like another actor. To me, E.T. was always a boy. He was very innocent, and one thing I tried to avoid was making him look old. For instance, the wrinkles on his face were designed to be like ornaments and nothing like wrinkles on the face of a human being. I just wanted him to look like a happy face.

I remember going to see *E.T.* at the Cineramadome with my (Italian) family when it came out. It was just phenomenal, and I was very excited to win my second Oscar for this film, which I shared with ILM. And it's a thrill that twenty years later *E.T.* feels like a new movie.

— Carlo Rambaldi, E.T. Creator

Carlo did a number of versions in clay, and I worked with him. I'm not an artist, so I didn't touch the clay but I would say, "Too scary. Too Disney. Too sweet."

Finally, this creature emerged from clay which, after a couple of weeks, became E.T.
—STEVEN SPIELBERG

LEFT: Carlo Rambaldi adjusting E.T.'s mouth for the filming of the scene in Elliott's room. ABOVE: Workroom with several versions of the E.T. costume.

21

Details and measurements of the different sections of the E.T. costume. BOTTOM RIGHT: *An E.T. technician working with the creature during the filming of the movie.*

The Eyes

The eyes of Albert Einstein...

...Ernest Hemingway...

...and Carl Sandburg.

I remember showing Carlo some pictures of Albert Einstein, Ernest Hemingway and Carl Sandburg. I loved their eyes and wanted E.T.'s eyes to be as frivolous and wizened and sad as those three icons.

I was not happy with any of the eye work that we were doing on E.T. The eyes looked like they were painted and didn't have any depth or authenticity. I kept saying, "Who does glass eyes?" Glass eyes look real. You can only spot the glass one because it stays fixed and the real one wanders. I asked Kathy to find somebody who makes glass eyes and give them a job working on E.T.

Kathy found Beverly Hoffman, who worked at the Jules Stein Eye Institute. Beverly came on board and did a wonderful job making over-sized glass eyes for us.

—STEVEN SPIELBERG

BELOW: E.T.'s eyes were spaced so far apart that the kid actors could only look in one eye at a time. They decided they would all look in the same eye at the same time and, for different scenes, choose alternate eyes.

BELOW: Carlo Rambaldi works on the skull of E.T. OPPOSITE: Sketches showing the expressions of E.T.'s nose, eyes, and brow and how they should move.

F. NOSE

① ② NOSTRILS FLARE OPEN AND RAISE UP WHEN E.T. IS SMELLING SOMETHING...

NOSTRILS CLOSE... AND MOVE SIDE TO SIDE AND DOWN....

FULL NOSE RAISES UP INTO A SQUINT...

4. EYES

EYEBALLS ALWAYS TRACK IN UNISON... FULL ROTATION IN SOCKETS... EYES ALWAYS APPEAR WET...

① SKIN UNDER AND ABOVE THE EYELID IS WRINKLED AND CAN CAUSE SQUINTING...
② EYELIDS CAN BLINK VERY FAST!!

EYES OPEN VERY WIDE IN SURPRISE... FOREHEAD GOES WAY BACK... LOWER LIDS DROP...

G. CONT.

① ② PUPILS DIALATE IN STRONG LITE...

EITHER EYE CAN WINK OR BOTH CAN CLOSE TO SQUINT AT SOMETHING... LIKE A BRIGHT LITE...

BOTH EYES CAN FULLY CLOSE IN A RELAXED SLEEPING POSITION...

H. BROW

BOTH BROWS RISE IN UNISON...

LEFT SIDE RISES INDEPENDENTLY..

RIGHT SIDE RISES INDEPENDENTLY...

RIGHT SIDE OF LEFT HALF...

LEFT SIDE OF RIGHT HALF

LEFT SIDE OF LEFT HALF

old. I told him we needed to test the creature. I asked Harold to bring Rachel to Carlo's shop, and he said okay.

By the time he arrived, this four-year-old was hysterically crying and was not into doing this at all. Harold says to me, "I don't know if this is going to work, I've tried to bribe her with two McDonald's burgers but it's not working. She doesn't want to do it."

I went over and talked to Rachel. She calmed down a little bit and got into the suit. But by the time we get the head on, she is completely hysterical again. She's jumping up and down and screaming and crying. Harold said, "Just roll tape."

So we roll tape and end up having to show Steven this hysterical, crying four-year-old in the suit.

But he bought it. He said, "Okay, this may be the way we have to go."

—KATHLEEN KENNEDY

E.T. Walks

We did get to a point where I finally threw up my hands and said, "I don't know how in the world we're ever going to get E.T. to move in a believable way, without putting somebody in a suit."

I knew Steven would never agree unless we could show him that it would work. I thought that if I could videotape somebody in a suit maybe I could show Steven that it works on some level. We certainly didn't have to rely solely on this, but we could use it for some shots at least.

So I called Harold Brown, Steven's attorney, because, at the time, his daughter was four years

FROM STANDING... INTO... SQUATING POSITION... SITTING... ON KNEES...

OPPOSITE: Two of the actors inside the creature: Pat Bilon (above) and Tamara De Treaux (below). Bilon was 2'10" tall and weighed 45 pounds. De Treaux was an actress from Los Angeles, while Bilon was a former sheriff's dispatcher from Youngstown, Ohio. ABOVE RIGHT: Steven Spielberg and E.T. during filming. LEFT: Initial sketches of E.T. sitting down from a standing position. In these early sketches E.T. had long legs. In the final design, the creature had short, squat legs, as shown in the top left photo.

I remember saying to Carlo Rambaldi that E.T. should kind of waddle when he walks like Chaplin with his cane. He should also look like Bambi slipping on the ice, where Bambi couldn't find his footing. When E.T. starts to walk on earth, he is ungainly and insecure.

Pat Bilon made the strongest contributions to E.T.'s walking scenes. But there were other people who also contributed. A wonderful young boy, Matthew De Meritt, who didn't have legs, was able to walk on his hands. He did the most memorable sequence when E.T. walks into the room, having had a few too many beers, and stumbles and falls on his face. Then Gertie knocks him over when she opens the refrigerator door and he falls over backwards. All of these were Matthew's contributions.

Tamara De Treaux did the very opening scene where E.T. comes out of the woodshed and places the Reese's Pieces on Elliott's sleeping bag. Tamara also did the last scene in the movie, where E.T. walks up the gangway, holding the flowers from Gertie.
—STEVEN SPIELBERG

LEFT: On the set during the filming of the opening scenes where the extraterrestrials are researching the plant life in the California hills. ABOVE: An actor on the 1981 set being fit with the E.T. suit.

Inside E.T.

I wanted to be able to see inside E.T. I wanted to see his organs when he turns on his heart light. I thought the organs should be moving in a strange way and we should see E.T. breathing. I think it was Craig Reardon who said, "I understand from your script that you think E.T. is a plant."

I said, "I don't think he's a mammal, he's not a bird, he's not a fish. I think he's a vegetable."

They suggested this concept of making E.T.'s insides look like a plant. I thought that was fantastic and they went ahead with that idea.

—STEVEN SPIELBERG

Three E.T.s

During the filming, three different types of E.T.s were used. The models and the different heads cost about $1,400,000. The electronic parts accounted for about $400,000 of that amount.

1) A MECHANICAL MODEL: The mechanical E.T. was operated by twelve men who were connected to the model by twenty-foot cables. Each operator controlled a different function on the model. Four people controlled the face alone. Spielberg called the operators, "E.T.'s Twelve Hearts."

2) AN ELECTRONIC MODEL: This model was operated by radio control. Both the electronic and the mechanical model had eighty-seven points of movement including ten points in the face alone.

3) E.T. SUITS: Actors were put inside costumes for the walking scenes, and a mime wore E.T. gloves for specific scenes involving his hands and arms.

MEMORANDUM

EXTRA-TERRESTRIAL PRODUCTIONS
Culver City, California

Mr. Carlo Rambaldi
Northridge, California 91324

RE: RED LIGHT – E.T.   1st July 1981

If you will recall, Steven has always empha-sized that the heart light should be organic, have depth and movement and the light should have the characteristics of a bright fluoroscope.

I should also mention that Steven up until now expected all E.T.'s to have the red light capability. If that is not possible, I will need to let him know his limitations right away.

Thank you.

Yours sincerely,
KATHY KENNEDY

MEMORANDUM

EXTRA-TERRESTRIAL PRODUCTIONS
Culver City, California

FROM: Ed Verreaux
TO: Craig Reardon
DATE: July 31, 1981
SUBJECT: E.T. HEART LIGHT

Aside from color:

A) Since this is an animated effect, light intensity should be variable according to conditions. . . .it shouldn't just snap on like a light switch but rather be able to increase or decrease in brightness from very dim (very slight like a light sunburn) to very bright (shining through the hospital bed sheets. . . hiding from Keys and his men in the ditch) and any position in between.

B) While E.T.'s skin is not totally transparent in the heart light area, we should be able to see some internal organ activity (always movement) when the light is on. The pulsing of the heart (two-three hearts?), intestinal contraction, changes in the density of viscera, lung expansions and contractions. The rib cage will block out light but the skin should be diffuse enough to allow some light to bleed through. Also, we should be able to see some vein activity in front of the light radiating out toward the limbs, not necessarily with bubbles of E.T.'s blood pumping through, but some lines to indicate blood vessels.

If you have any questions, please call me at the office.

Best regards,
ED VERREAUX

cc: Kathy Kennedy, Melissa Mathison, Steven Spielberg, Mitch Suskin

---

BELOW: Four of the dozen operators (Steven Spielberg called them "E.T.'s Twelve Hearts") working in unison to bring life to the creature.

Almost every member of the cast and crew wanted a portrait with the star of the movie. THIS PAGE: Among those who posed with E.T. are Carlo Rambaldi (26A) lighting a politically incorrect cigarette for the alien. OPPOSITE PAGE: Allen Davian (25A), Robert Macnaughton (29A), and Henry Thomas (23A)

ASSEMBLING the CAST

Casting ELLIOTT

I think, in a funny way, with children, you almost know the minute they walk into the room whether you're in fact looking at the character, because they do come in and claim the role in some way. Usually that's because you're casting some element of their existing personality. And that's what you're looking for in terms of trying to find the character.

—KATHLEEN KENNEDY

I could not find an Elliott. I looked for a long time, at least six months. Actually, I made an offer to a boy who I thought was Elliott, but that fell through. I was really only about a month away from shooting the movie and still did not have an Elliott.

Then I heard from Jack Fisk. He had just made a movie called *Raggedy Man* and he used this kid named Henry Thomas. Jack recommended Henry to our casting person.

—STEVEN SPIELBERG

My audition was kind of scary. I was reading these two random scenes, but I hadn't read the whole script and I didn't even know the story. So I read these two pages three or four times, and it was really bad. I remember thinking, I'm not reading very well. This is horrible, I'm not going to get this part.

Steven said we should do an improvisation. Here's the situation: You just found this creature and you love it. It's like your dog. It's your pet and the government wants to take it away from you and do experiments on him.

—HENRY THOMAS

I got behind the video camera, turned it on, and that's how Henry convinced me that he was Elliott. Everybody in the room was in tears. I just remember turning to Henry and saying, "Okay, kid, you got the part."

—STEVEN SPIELBERG

ABOVE: Henry Thomas poses with E.T. and his mom.
OPPOSITE: Drew Barrymore rides atop Steven Spielberg's shoulders during filming.

Casting GERTIE

I auditioned for *Poltergeist* and Steven said, "No, you're not right for this, you're right for this other movie. So come back."

I came in a lot of times. I was so happy to have a grown-up who listened to me talk. He believed in my stories; he loved them. It made me feel so good and so alive.

—DREW BARRYMORE

I met a lot of Gerties, but Drew had the part the minute she stepped into the room.

She began making up these stories that she was a punk rocker, she had a punk rock band, and she was going on the road. She's six years old and she's telling me that she's going to do a twenty-city tour in America with her punk rock band. Her stories kept getting bigger and bigger and wilder and wilder. She just blew me away. I mean, there was no second choice.

—STEVEN SPIELBERG

Casting Elliott's BIG BROTHER

W hen I first heard of E.T., it was called *A Boy's Life*. I was doing a play in New York at the time, and I came to L.A. to read for a movie called *The Entity*. I didn't get that part, but the casting director mentioned that there was something going on over at Spielberg's office. I ended up getting in on a late audition. I remember the day of the audition because it wasn't really an audition. They wouldn't allow the script to be seen. So it was more of an interview with Steven himself.

—ROBERT MACNAUGHTON

I thought Robert was a really good actor. He had stage experience and was the most professional of all the kids. He was the anchor because he had worked and acted before in front of people. He was really solid.

—STEVEN SPIELBERG

Casting KEYS

The first time I met Steven, I was brought in by a casting agent named Mike Fenton who really helped me at the start of my career. Mike wanted me to meet Steven for Indiana Jones.

Mike asked me if I could wear a hat. I said, "I wear hats all the time." So he gave me this fedora and said that I was going to be a swashbuckling adventurer. He said I should just go in and meet Steven.

I walked into the room and tripped over a lamp stand.

—PETER COYOTE

Casting MOM

If *Raiders* was a comedy, I would've cast Peter Coyote to play Indiana Jones because he was kind of awkward and clumsy. But he made a good impression on me because I remembered him.

When we were casting the part of Keys, I said, "Whatever happened to that guy that kept knocking things down when he came into audition for me and George [Lucas] for *Raiders*?"

I gave him the part.

—STEVEN SPIELBERG

Steven is a master at casting. He watches people and has a real talent for taking their quality and putting them in the role that's right for them. He originally saw me doing hookers and call girls and put me into his mother.

—DEE WALLACE STONE

I chose Dee Wallace because Dee was like a kid herself. I didn't feel I was violating my rule not to have adults in the film until the very end.

—STEVEN SPIELBERG

PART TWO:
A BOY'S LIFE
The Annotated, Illustrated Screenplay

The view comes to rest on a freak clearing, a barren meadow, nestled among the towering trees.

It is here that we see the spaceship.

END MAIN TITLES

EXT. THE LANDING SITE – NIGHT

The spaceship is not large. It slightly resembles a reflective hot-air balloon, a Christmas tree ornament, inscribed with a delicate gothic design. An open hatch door stretches down to the landing site. Soft pastel light spills from the interior of the ship, and in this light, we make out the *movements of creatures*.

The creatures are short, stocky, humanoid, but our distance and the misty atmosphere prevent any close identification of features. The creatures are banded together, working with strange, antiquated tools, probing the earth. *Their jerky movements and their reaction to the slightest sound reveal their hesitancy and fear.*

A smoky, camouflaging mist seems to emanate from the creatures themselves, on an inhale-exhale rhythm, as if their hot breath was consolidating in the cool night air, blanketing their tracks with fog.

A creature moves up the gangplank as we follow two creatures as they move along.

Another creature moves up the gangplank, and we see creatures' hands reach up and pull on a branch.

The Space Program

E.T. is my response to the stalled space program. If the government won't fund the space program, to allow people's imagination to soar, then all I can do is make movies that bring space down to earth and make it more accessible to the imagination.

—STEVEN SPIELBERG, 1981

LEFT: Henry Thomas in the Halloween scene when the movie was still known as A Boy's Life. *ABOVE: Charlie Bailey, chief model maker responsible for the spaceship. BELOW: Drawing by Ralph McQuarrie.*

45

Drawing by Ed Verreaux of the spaceship landing on earth.

PRODUCTION NOTES

Ideas for the Landing of the Spaceship

1. Initially, one of the ideas was to have Elliott witness the landing, along with other people.

2. At one point, there was talk of adding another character to the movie, a kind of Mr. Wizard, who would also see the ship and be the one adult who believes Elliott.

3. Steven Spielberg thought the ship could land in a vacant lot, but Melissa Mathison thought a forest would be more magical.

4. The opening scene was shot in the redwood forest area near Crescent City in northern California. Hit hard with rain, the landing site was completely flooded and, at a new location that was found, cows ate all of the grass. Greenery was gathered from other locations to fake the bottle grass.

INT. SPACESHIP – NIGHT

A soft-white den of mist. We hear clearly now the unique breathing pattern of the creature as we see his obscured form enter the ship through plant branches.

We are in a greenhouse — a Gothic cathedral of a structure. Heavy precipitation drips from the strange and varied plants. The creature moves toward the far end of the greenhouse.

EXT. THE LANDING SITE – NIGHT

An owl hoots. The creatures freeze. The danger passes. Work is resumed.

A SAPLING – NIGHT

On the ground in front of ferns, a tiny sapling stands. A creature's hands uproots it and moves it out of sight.

EXT. FOREST – NIGHT

THE CREATURE
The creature walks into the forest. His heart also begins to shine through, and the ruby glow pinpoints

Inside the Spaceship

1. An elaborate sprinkler system was installed on the interior set so there was always a thin mist of water.

2. Gardening tools were designed but never used.

3. Flowers were designed for the ship including watermelon-like blossoms.

4. Steven Spielberg remembered a movie called *The Day of the Triffids* and asked production designer James D. Bissell to include one in this scene. He produced a four-foot foam latex figure with a moveable armature.

5. The lab contained two dueling, hand puppet cobra plants with whip-like antennas which were filmed but cut during editing.

him: a small awkward creature, alone in the gigantic redwood forest under a starry sky.

EXT. FOREST – NIGHT – POV

The sounds of the forest rise, and we see the height of the trees from the creature's POV as the creature moves deeper into the forest.

The creature moves along, looking up and around.

EXT. HILL LOOKOUT – NIGHT – POV

To the sound of heavy breathing and an awkward tread, we see the creature's hand reach out and pull back a leafy limb.

THE VIEW: THE SOURCE OF LIGHT – POV

The source of light — a suburban neighborhood, edging up against the base of the mountains and the border of the forest.

THE CREATURE

We cannot see his face. He turns his head to look down the road.

THE VIEW: THE SOURCE OF LIGHT – POV

A sea of yellow house lights lies below him.

LEFT: Steven Spielberg directing a scene from the beginning of the film.

THE CREATURE

Following his reaction, we hear the sound of a motor, and with no further warning, harsh blinding white lights streak around the corner.

THE APPROACHING CAR pulls to a stop. The creature runs across the road, partially hidden by the forest ferns.

MORE CARS
converge on the scene. We see bright headlights. The creature hidden in a clump of ferns looks on, as we hear the slamming of doors and muffled voices.

A PUDDLE OF WATER
just in front of where the creature stands hidden. The feet of the moving men step into the puddle as they move past him.

NEAR A VEHICLE
We see a man step out. Seen only from the waist down, a ring of keys hangs from his belt. The keys make a tremendous racket, displacing all other sounds of the night. He moves to where the other men stand hovering over the map on the hood of a car.

EXT. THE LANDING SITE – NIGHT

The ship is looking deserted. All hands are on board.

The fellow creature remains in the door opening, his heart light sending frantic signals into the dark forest.

THE CREATURE
His red light comes on as he watches. His hand moves in to cover it.

EXT. THE FOREST – NIGHT

The men turn toward the clump of ferns the creature is standing in, and with their flashlights lighting their way, move toward his hiding place. Again we hear the sound of keys.

The creature moves quickly zigzagging invisibly through the tall ferns.

The movement alerts the men, and they move in the direction of it, flashlights sweeping everywhere.

Lights start flashing in the spaceship.

We see the creature gliding through the forest ferns, his ruby-red beacon throbbing.

The men are not far behind.

The chase continues; the creature leads the way.

CREATURE'S POV

The ferns in his foreground are lit by his own light part in his path. The men follow persistently.

Back in the spaceship, a creature waits; his heart light beaming.

They are on his trail. One man jumps through a V-shaped tree, taking the lead as the other men follow, flashing their lights.

The man with the keys moves amid the other men. His keys jangle horrifically as they move forward.

The creature is nearing the landing site. He crosses a road. All we can see is his red light signaling his position to his pursuers, as he moves into another part of the forest.

The pursuers continue their chase.

The landing site is almost in view. He races toward it, the men hot on his heels.

CREATURE'S POV

Again the ferns part as he races toward the ship.

EXT. THE LANDING SITE – NIGHT

The hatch door lifts. The last image from the interior of the ship is the fellow creature's red light as the door closes and we hear a panicked group breath.

SLOPE NEAR THE LANDING SITE (WHERE THERE IS A GATE)

The creature almost flies down the slope he is moving so rapidly.

EXT. THE LANDING SITE – NIGHT

The ship hovers, then departs quickly, spinning above the treetops and disappearing into the night sky.

SLOPE NEAR THE LANDING SITE

The men come racing toward the light. They stop and raise their flashlights to the sky. They move forward still hoping to find whatever it was they were following.

CLOSER: THE CREATURE

The creature stands. The creature cries out — a sound of desperation, disbelief, and fear.

SLOPE NEAR THE LANDING SITE

The creature stranded on earth moves back up the slope toward the forest, looking around at his new planet. He moves down toward the suburban lights.

THE MEN
move into the area where the ship had been frantically looking about, flashing flashlights.

INT. ELLIOTT'S HOUSE – NIGHT

CAMERA has pulled back now, REVEALING four boys seated around a kitchen table. They are into the final hours of late night "fantasy role-playing game." The table is cluttered with pop cans, potato chips, calculators, books, and a domino maze which is being used to signify the route of tonight's adventure.

MICHAEL – fourteen, tall, lanky. The oldest of the three children who live in this home.

Ideas Cut from the Script

Melissa Mathison and Steven Spielberg had many, many ideas for the script and here are a few that they ultimately rejected:

1) E.T. goes into a fox den and sees several cubs and their mother.

2) It's a belt, not a heart light, that lights up.

3) Elliott's father is in the movie.

4) Elliott tries to bait E.T. with Reddi-wip.

5) At a football game, E.T. gives Michael the power to win big.

6) Mom meets E.T. when Elliott gives him a shower.

7) There's a character in the movie named Mr. Pfister, a Mr. Wizard type, who helps the kids.

8) There's a character in the movie named Lance, an evil kid who wants to make a profit from E.T. Melissa Mathison was thinking that Lance would be Elliott's alter ego.

9) E.T. has a little pouch, like a kangaroo, and carries stuff around with him.

10) There's a parrot in the house who knows how to talk. The kids teach E.T. to talk the same way they taught the parrot and, when E.T. does finally speak, the mom thinks it is the parrot.

11) Harvey, the dog, gets hit by a car and E.T. heals him.

12) E.T. heals the J.R. character on the television show "Dallas."

ABOVE: E.T. was acclaimed for its realistic portrayal of family life and the conflicts between family members.

TYLER – Michael's friend, cute, sassy, wise beyond
his years.

STEVE – the game master, meticulous, inscrutable.

GREG – on the phone.

A fifth boy stands behind the bar by the table. He is
Elliott, nine or ten.

ELLIOTT

Steve.

STEVE

Five.

MICHAEL

Oh, great.

ELLIOTT

Steve.

STEVE

So you got an arrow right in your chest,
and you're out ten more rounds. Ten
more rounds.

ELLIOTT

I'm ready to play.

TYLER

Oh, no.

The boy, Elliott, is trying to get a word in. He is being
ignored.

GREG

Don't worry about it, Mike. I got resurrection. I'll bring you back.

ELLIOTT

I'm ready to play, Steve.

MICHAEL

I'm already one of the undead, Greg. I
can still throw death spells, huh, Steve?

GREG

I'm just trying to help you out, man.
Don't be so cranky.

STEVE

Yeah.

ELLIOTT

Steve.

TYLER

Hows 'bout throwing a spell over the
pizza man? Where's our pizza, man?
Get it? Huh?

Elliott has waited long enough. He interrupts finally.

ELLIOTT

Well, I'm ready now to play.

STEVE

You can't have a fight now. You're a thief.

TYLER

But I haven't gone yet.

ELLIOTT

I'm ready to play now, you guys!

STEVE

It's coming around to you.

GREG

We're in the middle, Elliott. You can't
just join any universe in the middle. I got
him! I got him! Mm. Hey, what am I ask-
ing him for, you guys?

MICHAEL

Did you say ten more rounds?

TYLER

"Papa Oom Mow Mow."

MICHAEL

"Papa Oom Mow Mow."

GREG

Mm-hm. All right. Okay. (*into telephone*) "Papa Oom Mow Mow." Yeah.

MICHAEL

Ten more rounds.

GREG

Yeah.

ELLIOTT

Mike?

GREG

I know. It's not for us. It's for his mother.

ELLIOTT

Mike?

GREG

"Papa Oom Mow Mow."

MICHAEL

You have to ask Steve. He's game master. He has absolute power.

GREG

"Papa Oom Mow Mow."

ELLIOTT

Steve?

GREG

Thanks a lot. Okay, bye.

TYLER

Steve, can I play now?

STEVE

Go wait for the pizza first.

ELLIOTT

Then I'm in?

STEVE

Yeah, you're in. But figure out your strategy, 'cause you're playing after Greg.

GREG

With plenty of sausage and pepperonis!

TYLER
Everything but the little fishies.

EXT. FRONT OF ELLIOTT'S HOUSE – NIGHT

Elliott stands in the driveway playing with a baseball. He has a mitt on. His house is at the top of a cul-de-sac, the last house before the onslaught of forest and mountains. A Volkswagen pulls up next to him.

ELLIOTT meets the Volkswagen and collects the pizza.

Elliott climbs the driveway, balancing the pizza on one hand.

EXT. FRONT YARD – NIGHT

As he heads for the door, there is a sudden, loud, crashing noise from the backyard.

Elliott halts.

ELLIOTT
Harvey? Harvey, is that you, boy?

The Music

Steven Spielberg made *Close Encounters of the Third Kind* about four years before *E.T.* and, in the broadest sense, they have similar themes. I think that what makes them both successful is that they affirm the fact that we are not alone in the universe. In the case of *Close Encounters*, the beginning of the film is much more terrifying because we don't know who these aliens are. But there's a great kind of uplifting feeling of almost religiosity, I think, at the end when we suddenly recognize that we have brothers and sisters. And so, there's a relief in the music. *E.T.* is also a bit scary in the beginning, but the minute we meet this little creature, the film becomes much more of a love story. That makes for a very different kind of musical challenge in *E.T.* as compared with *Close Encounters*.

Music is, of course, very difficult to verbalize for all of us. I could just parenthetically point out something that we've all been told but it can bear repeating. The one thing that perhaps every culture on earth shares, even before language, is music. When tribes couldn't speak to each other, they would beat a drum to organize a war or sing a song to

ABOVE: John Williams and the star of E.T. at a concert.

celebrate a birth, or wail something at a funeral. There's a very basic human, non-verbal aspect to our need to make music and use it as part of our human expression. It doesn't have to do with body movements, it doesn't have to do with articulation of a language, but with something spiritual. So, for a composer like myself and a director like Steven Spielberg, it's very difficult to say: "What do we really want?" The simplest answer about my relationship with Steven Spielberg is that we talk a lot and we talk about tempo, not so much in a harmonic or melodic context, but how fast or how slow the music should be. Tempo is the first thing a composer has to get right. The next thing has to do with how loud or how soft the music should be. Then, we determine the harmonic ambiance and talk about emotion and texture.

—JOHN WILLIAMS

INT. KITCHEN – NIGHT

Mary moves with some dishes from the stove to the dishwasher. She is swaying with the music as she bends over to put the dishes into the dishwasher.

MICHAEL
Oh, this is really great, Ty, you destroyed the dungeon. Thank you.

GREG
Is this the one I asked for?

STEVE
Yeah, that's the one you asked for.

GREG
Yeah.

MICHAEL
Stop it!

GREG
All right.

TYLER
Sorry.

EXT. BACKYARD – NIGHT

Elliott continues calling his dog until he reaches the backyard. A roomy, grassy stretch of land with a vegetable garden and a lattice toolshed. A red light is hanging over the fence gate. The gate is blowing in the wind. We hear what sounds like a sharp inhalation and see what looks like a sucking of mist through the toolshed door.

ELLIOTT
Harvey?

Elliott walks to the tool shed. He stops and puts the pizza on the ground, then throws the baseball into the toolshed. Wait a beat, then the ball comes hurtling back out at him.

Elliott, turns to run, trips over the pizza, and continues toward the back door.

INT. KITCHEN – NIGHT

Mary has turned to the table. Her hand on her hip.

TYLER
All's you can get is those forty-year-olds.

MARY
So, how do you win this game, anyway?

GREG
Fine. So who got Lisa last year, huh?

STEVE
There's no winning. It's like life. You don't win at life.

GREG
Money helps.

STEVE
Yeah, but....

ELLIOTT
Mom! Mom! There's something out—!

TYLER
All right. Where's the pizza?

ELLIOTT
Mom! Mom! There's something out there!

MARY
Hey, now...

ELLIOTT
It's in the...

MARY
...calm down. Calm down.

ELLIOTT
...toolshed! It threw the ball at me.

TYLER
There's something out there. Mom, Mom.

GREG
Yeah, I know where it can go.

MARY

Cool it.

TYLER

It threw the ball at...at me.

ELLIOTT

Quiet! Nobody go out there.

MARY

Stop now! You guys stay right here!

All the boys are now intent on defying Elliott. They rise to move outside. Greg and Tyler take a knife from near the stove and move out. Steve is in the lead. They continue out. Michael passing his mother says:

MICHAEL

You stay here, Mom. We'll check it out!

MARY

And put those knives back!

ELLIOTT

Come on, Mom. Mom, I swear, there was something there.

MARY

Okay, Elliott.

ELLIOTT

It's out in the… toolshed.

MARY

I'll get the flashlight. Hold it. Wait a... minute, come on.

As they all go toward the door, Mary and Elliott move behind them.

ELLIOTT

Mom.

GREG

You little creep. Creepy.

EXT. BACKYARD – NIGHT

The army of boys are on the patio. Mary takes the lead with Elliott beside her.

MARY

What exactly did you see?

TYLER

It's dark out here.

ELLIOTT

It's in there.

STEVE

It's scary.

MARY

There's nothing in here.

MICHAEL

The gate's open.

Tyler moves into the toolshed and kneels, noticing something.

TYLER

Look at these.

Michael too crosses in as Mary shines the light on some odd footprints.

MICHAEL (*on his knee*)

The coyote's come back again, Mom.

MARY

Okay, party's over. Everybody back inside. Get out. Hurry up. Quick. Hurry up. Come on. Tyler, give me that knife.

ABOVE: Steven Spielberg and Henry Thomas working on the scene where Elliott throws his ball into the shed and E.T. throws it back.

Tyler gives her the knife, and kneels to the pizza, opening it and taking a piece from the box and standing.

TYLER
Oh, great. Nice one, Elliott.

ELLIOTT
I–It was an accident.

TYLER
Yeah, accident.

MARY
A pizza? Who said you guys could order a pizza? Huh?

ELLIOTT
Uh, h–him, he—

GREG
Uh, I, but—

She shoos them all toward the house.

MARY
Huh? In the house.

TYLER
You geek, man.

MICHAEL
Hey, Greg.

Elliott, beside Mary.

ELLIOTT
But, Mom, it was real. I swear.

MARY
I know, I know.

TYLER
Douche bag, Elliott.

MARY
(*gently hitting the back of Tyler's head*)
No "douche bag" talk in my house!

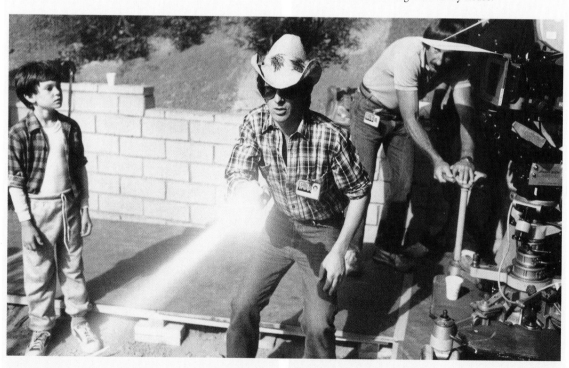

ABOVE: Steven Spielberg directs Henry Thomas in the backyard scene.

LEFT: E.T. as he appeared in the 1982 release. ABOVE: For the 2002 release, the creature's features were enhanced.

ELLIOTT

There was something. I swear.

MARY

I know...

They continue toward the door.

The toolshed is quiet; suddenly a hand comes out and holds on to the doorjamb.

INT. ELLIOTT'S ROOM – NIGHT

The clock on the stand beside Elliott's bed reads 2:01 A.M. CAM PANS to Harvey asleep in the lower bunk. A sound is heard, and Harvey reacts to it. He stands and looks toward the window. CAM PANS to upper bunk, and we see Elliott also awake looking toward the sound of the noise outside the window.

EXT. BACKYARD – NIGHT

Elliott descends steps at the back of the house and turns toward garden. Elliott moves cautiously into the yard holding a lit flashlight, muttering and whistling to himself in fear.

He approaches the vegetable garden, coming from the side of the house. He moves through a row of cornstalks, looking around from side to side.

ELLIOTT

Elliott, you're crazy.

He hears a soft crushing sound, and is momentarily startled. He continues on. He turns, and then he notices the footprints. He follows them until they come to an abrupt end. He is staring at a clump of cornstalks. He gently pulls them apart, and shines the flashlight between them.

E.T.'s face comes bursting through the cornstalks.

It is a terrible sight, like nothing we have ever seen before. E.T.'s wide head is tightened back in leathery creases and furrows. His thick lips are parted in a horrible grimace. His large round eyes are wide, the pupils dilated to an enormous size. Tiny teeth are bared as E.T. makes a terrifying sound — an imitative noise — the SOUND OF KEYS.

Elliott screams and hits the ground. The flashlight rolls to the side, flashing a light across his face.

He sees the movement of the cornstalks as though something were passing by them, but cannot see E.T. again. He rises.

ELLIOTT carefully moves out of the garden toward the hill and back gate. The swings are moving, but E.T. is gone.

MARY

If you ever see it again, whatever it is, don't touch it. Just...call me, and I'll have somebody come and take it away.

GERTIE

Like the dogcatcher?

ELLIOTT

But they'll give it a lobotomy or do experiments on it or something.

MARY

It's your turn to do the dishes, fellas.

MICHAEL

I set and cleared.

ELLIOTT

I set and cleared.

MICHAEL

I did breakfast.

GERTIE

I did breakfast.

MICHAEL

What's the matter, Mom?

MARY

He hates Mexico.

Mary starts to leave the kitchen; she is in tears.

MICHAEL

Damn it! Why don't you...grow up? Think how other people feel for a change!

Elliott takes his plate from the table and almost throws it into the sink. He turns the hot water on. Steam covers the window as Elliott stares through it.

EXT. BACKYARD – NIGHT

Elliott sits, wrapped in his bag, in the lounge chair asleep. His flashlight is still lit.

CLOSE ON ELLIOTT sound asleep. His eyes are open, and he looks toward the toolshed.

He sees a shadow approaching.

He sits up.

ON E.T.

He is now at the toolshed entrance and slowly moving toward Elliott. His face is soft now, his eyes wide and gentle, his mouth closed.

E.T. stares at the boy. The boy has wide eyes and is staring back.

ELLIOTT
Mo–... Mom... Mom. Michael. Michael. Mom.

E.T. is near the lounge chair now, and his hand extends to the sleeping bag near Elliott's feet.

Elliott tries to scream, but only inaudible sounds come out.

Elliott recoils, then sees that E.T. has left something on the bag. He looks, shining his flashlight onto it. It is a Reese's Pieces candy.

INT. HALLWAY NEAR STAIRCASE – NIGHT

Elliott comes from the steps to the landing and lays down some Reese's Pieces. Elliott moves to the doorway of his room and kneels. E.T.'s hands reach for the candy. E.T. comes from the staircase and starts toward Elliott's room.

INT. ELLIOTT'S ROOM – NIGHT

Elliott enters his room and entices E.T. with more Reese's Pieces. E.T. takes them. Elliott's bag of Reese's Pieces is empty. He swiftly moves to the desk in his

SCRIPT NOTES

In the original scene, E.T. gives Elliott only one piece of candy. The hand dropping several pieces of candy was an insert shot, filmed after the end of principal photography.

Lighting: The Magic Look

One of the things Steven knew from the very beginning was that E.T. would be a very shadowy, hardly seen figure in the early stages of the film. We would take a while to discover him. So we had to decide: What color should he be? What texture should we make his skin, especially for the initial stages where we were to barely see the outline of this creature?

One of the things we tested was different colors. I remember him being everything from somewhat of a green to the much more purple color that he wound up.

E.T.'s brownish skin with purple overtones evolved out of those early tests. Initially, I was shooting footage of just the head, and I knew that Steven didn't want E.T. lit with too much detail. In those early stages, we evolved the procedure of using a strong back light on him, putting his face largely in shadow with just the glint in the eyes. And that was how we shot the beginning scenes of E.T., other than those brief glimpses with the flashlights in the cornstalks.

Once we had E.T.'s lighting down, we had to decide how to light the scene around him so that it all made sense. One of the first things I said when I read the script was that everything about the house, the neighborhood, and the family had to be very, very real without any false or mysterious feeling.

Everything had to be naturally motivated because the magic would happen only in the presence of E.T. When E.T. entered the house, the house would remain the same but the room or the closet would be transformed into this magic place.

—ALLEN DAVIAU, DIRECTOR OF PHOTOGRAPHY

LEFT: The film crew on location. Allen Daviau, director of photography, is on the far right.

room, searching the drawers for some new bait. He finds an apple and moves quickly back to the door.

E.T. is gone. Suddenly he spots his head and hands, and they are moving behind a table. Elliott scurries along with them, but E.T. upsets a box of pencils, and in throwing his hands back, knocks down a shelf from the shelves behind him.

Elliott runs to the door and closes it, listening a moment to hear whether he has wakened anyone. He sighs a sigh of relief and moves into the room.

E.T. is standing in a corner as Elliott moves into the room as close as he dares to go. Beside him is his bunk bed. He carefully pulls a blanket off the bottom bunk and throws it onto E.T. E.T. briefly reacts, but then feels the warmth of the blanket and pulls it around him.

We get a good look at him. He is three-and-a-half feet tall, and his thin arms, partially covered by the blanket, hang below his narrow hips. His belly is heavy, now covered by the blanket. His head is oblong and flat—some think like a turtle's. His eyes never leave Elliott.

ELLIOTT is astonished, looking at him curiously.

E.T. holding the blanket around him, looks back just as curious.

ELLIOTT scratches his nose and is astonished as E.T. scratches his nose.

ELLIOTT tries an experiment. He touches his mouth and the side of his head, and to his surprise, E.T. touches his mouth, then the side of his head.

ELLIOTT
Wow.

Elliott holds out all five fingers, E.T. holds out all four fingers. Elliott, one finger. E.T., one finger. Elliott rapidly crooks his finger twice; E.T. crooks the same finger. They continue this interrogation of each other until sleep begins to overtake them.

E.T.'s eyes become droopy. Elliott in turn swoons slightly. Trying not to take his eyes off E.T., Elliott moves back to an armchair and sits down, trying to keep his eyes open.

E.T.'s eyes are closed. Elliott falls completely asleep. E.T. opens his eyes and looks around his new surroundings.

EXT. FOREST LANDING SITE – NIGHT

The clearing is lit by lights. An ongoing clandestine operation. The earlier image of alien creatures gently probing the earth is replaced with the crude and lumbering movements of humans, scouring the area with a fine-tooth comb. Flash cameras briefly turn more light on. Portable machines churn and beep, displacing the rustle of leaves and the hum of nocturnal life. Infrared lights flash.

CLOSE ON KEYS

The keys jingle as he bends to the ground. His hand discovers something. It gives him pause.

CAMERA MOVES CLOSER

Keys unearths a few Reese's Pieces. He lifts one from the soil, and we can hear the crunch off camera. His flashlight goes out.

FADE IN:

INT. ELLIOTT'S ROOM – DAY

Elliott is lying on the top bunk bed. Mary takes a thermometer out of his mouth. Elliott appears to be desperately ill. She reads the thermometer.

MARY
Okay, you're hot. I'll be back.

She sticks the thermometer back into Elliott's mouth. She leaves the room. Elliott immediately takes the thermometer out of his mouth, swings a lamp closer to him, and takes the heating pad out from under the covers. He holds the thermometer to the light bulb heating it up, and holds the pad to his face making his face hot.

MICHAEL (*OC*)
Mary, can I back the car out?

MARY (*OC*)
Not one foot past the driveway.

Elliott hears her coming back and puts everything back in place.

MARY moves to the closet, opening the doors.

Villains:
Adults and Science

I drew upon the *Close Encounters* experience in having no alien villains whatsoever in that film. The alien visitation was to observe and not destroy. The villains in *E.T.* really should be the adults who do not have the same pure understanding that children have about a situation like this.

The adults would be more frightened than the kids and call the police. The police and the government would not understand at all and would want to experiment on the alien, do a vivisection or such.

So the villain in the story would be the adults and the threat would be science.

—Steven Spielberg

INT. CLOSET

Mary enters the closet.

EXT. FRONT OF HOUSE – DAY

Michael backs the car down the driveway, screeching to a noisy stop past the end of the driveway. He pulls back up into the driveway, just past the sidewalk.

INT. ELLIOTT'S ROOM – DAY

Elliott's face expresses panic as Mary shakes out the quilt. Relief — it is only a quilt. (VARIATION: Elliott is seated up, and the panic is expressed as the thermometer falls out of his mouth. He puts it back in his mouth when he sees it is only a quilt. He lies back down.)

Mary moves back to his side with the quilt.

INT. ELLIOTT'S ROOM – DAY

MARY
You were outside last night waiting for that thing to come back, weren't you? You gonna live if I go to work?

MARY
Okay. No T.V.

Elliott sighs with relief. Sure she has finally left, he gets out of bed and moves into the closet to check on E.T.'s whereabouts.

EXT. FRONT OF HOUSE – DAY

The car is in the driveway where Michael left it. Mary moves toward the car where Gertie is bending down looking at the skid marks Michael made. As her mother approaches her she rises, tattletaling.

MARY
Come on.

GERTIE
Mommy, look what Michael did. This and that and—

MARY
I see them, Gert, and when I catch him, I'll catch him.

She has opened the back door of the car for Gertie, who enters and immediately moves to the front seat.

INT. ELLIOTT'S ROOM – DAY

Elliott moves into the room from out of the closet. E.T. follows him. He has a blanket wrapped around him.

ELLIOTT
Come on. Don't be afraid. It's all right. Come on. Come on. Come on. Come on. Come on.

They stand looking at each other.

ELLIOTT
Do you talk? You know, talk?

E.T. is silent.

ELLIOTT
Me human. Boy. Elliott. Ell-ee-utt Elliott.

Silence. Then E.T. crosses to the table. Elliott follows and begins explaining things to him.

ELLIOTT
Coke, see? We drink it. It's, uh, it's a drink. You know... food. These are toys. These are little men. This is Greedo, and then this is Hammerhead. See. . . this is Walrus Man. And then this is Snaggletooth. And this is Lando Calrissian. See? And this is Boba Fett. And, look, they can even have wars. Look at this. And look, fish. The

Kid Talk

A lot of the kids found wonderful things to say that came from the truth of themselves and that they were able to put into the movie.

—STEVEN SPIELBERG

Steven wasn't afraid to let kids be kids and bring something new to the film. He had this table set up in Elliott's bedroom with all this junk on it — *Star Wars* toys and little gadgets and everything. He said, "Okay, you've brought E.T. to your room and now show him what's on your table. Go down the line and introduce everything you can."

—HENRY THOMAS

fish eat the fish food. And the shark eats the fish. But nobody eats a shark. See, this is Pez. Candy. See, you eat it. You put the candy in here, and then when you lift up the head, the candy comes out, and you can eat it! You want some? Oh. This is a peanut. You eat it. But you can't eat this one, 'cause this is fake. This is money. See? We put the money in the peanut. You see? Bank. You see? And then this is a car. This is what we get around in. You see? Car.

ELLIOTT
Hey! Hey, wait a second! No! You don't eat 'em. Are you hungry? I'm hungry. Stay.

Elliott moves toward the door.

ELLIOTT
Stay. I'll be right here. Okay? I'll be... right here.

SCRIPT NOTES

Melissa Mathison's favorite scene in the movie is here where Elliott shows E.T. his toys. All this dialogue was ad-libbed by Henry Thomas.

INT. ELLIOTT'S ROOM

Harvey starts to enters as Elliott opens the door.

ELLIOTT
Harv!

Elliott quickly bends down and holds the dog.

ELLIOTT
No bite! No bite! Come on, Harvey.

Elliott takes Harvey out with him and closes the door.

INT. KITCHEN

Elliott at the refrigerator.

ELLIOTT
He'll like this. This.

INT. ELLIOTT'S ROOM

Left to his devices, E.T. wanders to the umbrella stand. E.T. takes an umbrella out, and it springs open. He quickly drops it.

In the closet, a stuffed animal coyote falls over, and we see the umbrella spinning on the bedroom floor.

INT. KITCHEN – DAY

At the moment of E.T.'s fear of the umbrella, we cut to

Elliott, standing at the refrigerator. Elliott shrieks and drops a quart of milk and other things he is gathering from the refrigerator.

INT. ELLIOTT'S ROOM – DAY

Elliott moves to the closet.

INT. CLOSET – DAY

Elliott enters still holding the sandwiches and Cokes. He sees a pile of stuffed animals in a corner of the closet.

> **ELLIOTT**
> (*to the pile of stuffed animals*)
> Are you okay?

The animals fall to the floor in foreground of Elliott, revealing E.T. He is shaking.

> **ELLIOTT**
> Too much excitement, huh? You want
> a Coke?

INT. BATHROOM – DAY

CLOSE: A bathroom scale. We see E.T.'s feet on the scale. The reading is less than forty-five pounds. E.T. steps off.

Elliott is beside him, amazed at the reading.

> **ELLIOTT**
> Thirty-five pounds, thirty-five pounds!!!

E.T. moves to the sink; Elliott follows.

> **ELLIOTT**
> But you're so fat.

They stand at the sink, looking in the mirror. Elliott holds his hand over his own head, then over E.T.'s.

> **ELLIOTT**
> How tall are you? I must be four feet, six
> inches, you must be around three...

LEFT INSET: Melissa Mathison and Henry Thomas on the set of Elliott's house. As screenwriter/associate producer, Mathison also helped rehearse the kids.

Elliott's conversation falls off as E.T.'s neck comes up, making him taller. Elliott, amazed, examines his own neck, as well as E.T.'s.

Elliott moves over to the bathtub. He starts to explain the faucet and water, etc.

ELLIOTT
This is where the water comes from. You

see? This is hot, and this is cold. Now, it all comes from a big water tower. It goes through pipes, and sometimes dead bugs, they come through the pipes and land in the bath. But it's real sick. But, anyway, look.

He turns the water on. E.T. has found an opened bottle

ABOVE: The bathroom scene with E.T. and Elliott was cut from the original release of the film but added to the 2002 version. BELOW: Illustrations by Ed Verreaux of the creature's neck extension.

of perfume. He smells it and sneezes, dropping the bottle into the sink.

Elliott picks up a Coke that is on the tub and moves to E.T. near the sink, still looking in the mirror.

ELLIOTT
Are you thirsty? I am.

He opens the Coke, and it squirts all over his face. At that same moment, the telephone in Mary's room rings, surprising them both. Elliott still shocked from the Coke.

ELLIOTT
I'll get it.

He moves out of the bathroom.

INT. MARY'S ROOM – DAY

Elliott picks up the phone, and puts the Coke down on the nightstand.

ELLIOTT
Hi. Yeah, I'm fine. Sure. Yeah, I still got a fever, though. Yeah. Uh-huh.

He moves toward the door and opens it, checking on Harvey who sticks his nose in. Elliott quickly closes the door, keeping Harvey out in the hall.

ELLIOTT
Back. I'm fine, Mom. Yeah. Yeah.

He moves toward the nightstand again, trying to get off the phone. In his background, we can see E.T. in the bathroom move from the sink toward the tub. The blanket he is wearing falls off.

ELLIOTT
No. Mom, I've gotta get in bed now, okay? Good-bye. Mom...Mom, I'm sick. Mom, I don't need to go to the doctor!

INT. MARY'S ROOM – DAY

He moves once more toward the door. He is so intent on getting Mary off the phone that he does not see E.T. in his background fall into the tub, which is by now full of water because Elliott forgot to turn it off.

ELLIOTT
Mom, I only had a fever of ninety-nine today. Okay, and a half. Uh-huh. Yeah, Mom. Okay, bye. Mom, I've, I've gotta

BELOW: It's bath time for E.T., helped along by Steven Spielberg.

SCRIPT NOTES

This bathroom scene was deleted from the original cut of the movie. For the 2002 edition, this entire scene is reinstated. Many of the scenes were digitally enhanced for the new release (see page 174, The Restoration: An E.T. for 2002, for more details on the 2002 release).

throw up. Mom, please. I'm gonna throw up on the phone if...if you don't let me go. Okay, bye. Mom, I've gotta throw up now. Yeah, uh...

He picks up the Coke, pours its contents into the phone, and hangs up.

He moves back toward the bathroom.

INT. BATHROOM – DAY

We can see Elliott from the bathroom. We can also see E.T. under water. Elliott sees E.T. He runs to him, terrified. He pulls him up out of the water.

> **ELLIOTT**
> You could drown in stuff like this.

E.T. pushes Elliott's arm off of him and falls back into the water enjoying it.

> **ELLIOTT**
> Is this your idea of a good time?

INT. KITCHEN – DAY

Michael, wearing his football shoulder pads, enters singing from the playroom. He opens the refrigerator door, takes out a Coke, and continues singing as he exits the kitchen.

> SCRIPT NOTES
>
> The scenes of Elliott giving E.T. a bath were cut from the original 1982 release, and restored to the 2002 release.

INT. ELLIOTT'S ROOM – DAY

Elliott moves to the door of his room and opens it, admitting Michael. He steps back; Michael stays in the doorway.

> **ELLIOTT**
> Mike, Mike, come in.

> **MICHAEL**
> How you feelin', faker?

> **ELLIOTT**
> I'm feeling fine. Look, I've got something really important to tell you.

> **MICHAEL**
> You know what? Tyler said he got 69,000 on Asteroids yesterday. But he pulled the plug.

ELLIOTT

Look, remember the goblin?

MICHAEL

You're so lame, Elliott.

ELLIOTT

Come on, Michael, he came back.

MICHAEL

He came back? He came back?!
Oh, my God!

Michael pretends something is pulling his head out the door. His head reenters.

ELLIOTT

One thing!

ELLIOTT

I have absolute power. Say it. Say it.

MICHAEL

What have you got?

MICHAEL

Is it the coyote?

Elliott crosses to Michael, closes the door, and leads him to the center of the room, as he says:

ELLIOTT

No. Look. Okay, now...swear it. The most excellent promise you can make. Swear as my only brother, on our lives—

MICHAEL

Okay, don't get so heavy. I swear.

ELLIOTT

Okay, um, stand over there, and, um,
you'd better take off your shoulder pads.

He marches Michael over near the table, turning him so he can't see the closet door.

MICHAEL

What?!

ELLIOTT

You might scare him. And, um, close
your eyes.

(*as he enters the closet*)

MICHAEL

Don't push it, Elliott.

ELLIOTT

I'm not comin' out there until your eyes
are closed.

MICHAEL

Okay, they're closed. Mom is gonna kill you.

He moves toward the closet. Michael removes his shoulder pads.

ABOVE: Steven Spielberg and Henry Thomas rehearsing on set.

SCRIPT NOTES

The shot of Michael coming home from school was done after the end of principal photography with a stand-in for Robert Macnaughton.

SCRIPT NOTES

A stained glass window was added to the closet to indicate whether it was night or day. The closet, and other interior sets (Elliott's bedroom, the long hallway, Gertie's room and another closet) were all constructed on ten-inch elevated floors so that the cables for E.T. would not be in the way.

ELLIOTT
Okay, um, swear it one more time.
I have absolute—

MICHAEL
You have absolute power. Yes.

ELLIOTT and E.T. step out of the closet. Elliott puts his head on E.T.'s shoulder, and nods to the creature reassuringly. He looks to his brother again.

Michael slowly turns to look at what is behind him. He sees E.T. He is stunned. Suddenly the door flies open, and Gertie comes running in.

GERTIE
Elliott, look what I made for you.

She sees E.T. and starts to scream. E.T. screams. Elliott screams.

Then Michael screams and backs into the shelves on the wall, and they come tumbling down.

Elliott catches himself and yells.

ELLIOTT
Stop! Stop!

He moves quickly to Gertie, putting his hand over her mouth, and moves her away from E.T. Michael steps in near them. They hear their mother OC.

MARY
Kids, I'm home! Guys?! Is anybody up there?!

ELLIOTT
Get in the closet. Fast.

Gertie enters closet, followed by Michael, and then E.T. Gertie starts to scream again. Michael puts his hand over her mouth again. The door is closed.

INT. ELLIOTT'S ROOM – DAY

Elliott moves quickly toward the table near the door, and picks up the toy shark and pretends to play with it. Mary enters.

MARY
Anybody home?! Hi, honey, you fee—
What happened in here?

She looks around, spotting the shelves on the floor and the rest of the mess. Amazed.

ELLIOTT
Oh. You mean my room.

MARY
(looking around stunned)
This is no room. This is an accident.

ELLIOTT
I was, um, reorganizing.

MARY
I can see that. Put those shelves back on the wall, Elliott.

INT. CLOSET – DAY

Michael holds hand over Gertie's mouth, as they stare at E.T.

Mary heads toward the closet, picking up some clothes off a chair and moves toward Elliott. Mike and Gertie watch through the louvred door.

MARY
Let's get the toys off the floor. Make your bed, since you're not using it. Well, you're feeling better, I see. You guys, keep an eye on Gertie for me while I take a shower?

INT. ELLIOTT'S ROOM – DAY

Elliott nods. She kisses his forehead.

ELLIOTT

Absolutely.

ELLIOTT

Bye, Mom.

Mary leaves the room, and Elliott sighs relief, drops the shark on the floor, and walks toward the closet.

INT. CLOSET – DAY

Elliott enters, and moves toward E.T. Michael still has his hand over Gertie's mouth.

MICHAEL

Elliott ——

ELLIOTT

(*staring at E.T.*)
I'm keeping him.

GERTIE

(*her voice muffled because of Michael's hand*)
What is it?

ELLIOTT

He won't hurt you, Gertie. He won't hurt you, Gertie.

ELLIOTT

We're not gonna hurt you.

Michael removes his hand from her mouth as she begins to move toward Elliott and E.T. Michael moves in too.

GERTIE

Is he a boy or a girl?

She kneels before E.T.

ELLIOTT

He's a boy.

GERTIE

Was he wearing any clothes?

ELLIOTT

(*kneeling*)
No. But, look, you can't tell. Not even Mom.

GERTIE

Why not?

ELLIOTT

Because, um, grown-ups can't see him. Only little kids can see him.

Gertie looks unbelievingly at Elliott.

GERTIE

Gimme a break.

ELLIOTT

Well, do you know what's going to happen if you do tell?

He takes the doll she is holding from her and tosses it to Michael.

ELLIOTT

Do it, Mike. We have to.

Michael takes Gertie's doll, and pretends he is wrenching its arm off.

MICHAEL

(*in Mr. Bill voice*)
Oh, no, please, no! Don't make me! Please! Somebody help me! Help me!

Gertie runs to him, defending her doll. Gertie's eyes fill with terror.

MICHAEL

Nooo!

E.T. watches.

Michael gives her the doll back.

77

The Kids on Set

I hung out with Robert. I was like the little brother trying to follow the guy around which worked because that was the character in the beginning. Until I find the alien, nobody really wanted to be my friend.

—HENRY THOMAS

The thing with Drew worked out perfectly because that was supposed to be the relationship in the movie, you know, me torturing her doll or whatever. That's how we treated her. I'm very guilty about it.

—ROBERT MACNAUGHTON

We did have a lot of fun.

—DREW BARRYMORE

One of my jobs as associate producer and writer was to rehearse with the kids. It was great fun. They would catch me on misspellings or give me a bad time about some piece of dialogue, or come up with something they thought was better. I finally had to kind of show them who was boss and tell them that I was the writer, they were the kids and they had to do what I said.

—MELISSA MATHISON

LEFT: *The cast of kids and some of their stand-ins. Bottom right is Matthew De Meritt, the boy who is legless and appeared inside the E.T. costume.* BELOW: *The kids spent several hours a day with a teacher attending to their schoolwork.*

ELLIOTT
(*to Gertie*)
You promise?

GERTIE
Yes.

ELLIOTT
(*to Michael*) Do you promise?

They move toward E.T. again, kneeling before him.

EXT. OVERLOOK

Keys and his men with Geiger counters.

MARY'S ROOM

She moves into her bedroom and waters a plant in a corner, then moves back near the entrance to water another plant. Gertie comes out of her room in background of Mary. Mary sees her. Gertie is pulling a wagon.

MARY
What are you doing, Gert?

GERTIE
I'm going to play in Elliott's room.

MARY
Okay. Don't let him torture you.

GERTIE
I won't, Mary.

Mary moves out of the room.

GERTIE pauses, puts down the handle of her wagon, lifts the very unhappy geranium, and puts it into her wagon. Harvey is wandering around and moves to Elliott's door as Gertie approaches the door, too. She knocks three times.

INT. ELLIOTT'S ROOM – NIGHT

Michael lets Gertie in. Harvey butts his way in behind her. E.T. stands near a table with a huge plate of food before him. He is munching on watermelon and celery at the moment. Elliott across the table from him, looks curiously on.

Michael tries to hurry Gertie along.

MICHAEL
Come on. Come on. Hurry up.

GERTIE
Don't be so pushy, pushy.

With her wagon, she moves beside Elliott, and starts to unload it. She puts the geranium on the table in front of E.T.

GERTIE
A plant for you.

Gertie talks throughout.

MICHAEL
(*talking over her*)
Maybe he's some animal that wasn't supposed to live. You know, like those rabbits we saw that time.

ELLIOTT
Don't be lame.

GERTIE
(*as she puts the Play-Doh on the table*)
I brought you some clay. Green, orange, red.

MICHAEL
It could be a monkey, or, or an orangutan or something.

ELLIOTT
A bald monkey?

GERTIE
Is he a pig? He sure eats like one.

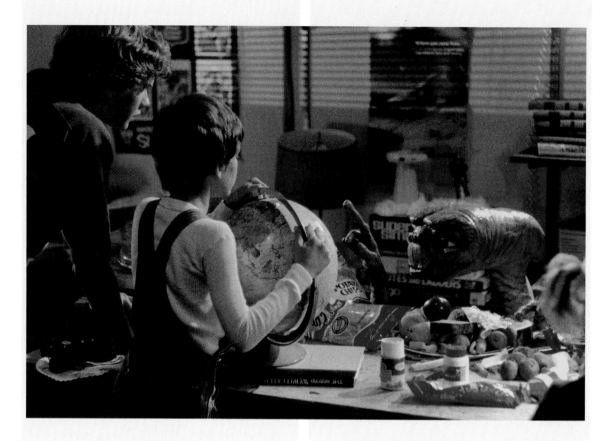

GERTIE
(*to E.T.*) You could make faces, and make
them mean and happy, and make them
get sharp teeth and bite you.

Michael moves to the nightstand beside Elliott's
bed, finds the atlas, and moves next to Elliott
with it. Elliott quickly finds a map of the United
States. He points.

ELLIOTT
We are here.

GERTIE
And you can make 'em have their head
cut off.

ELLIOTT
We're here.

MICHAEL
(*remembering the globe on Elliott's desk*)
No, use this.
(*he hands Elliott the globe*)

Elliott puts the atlas down, sets the globe
atop it, and points once again to the
United States.

ELLIOTT
Okay, we're here. We are here. Where are
you from?

E.T. looks at the globe. He points to the window.
Gertie looks under the table at his feet.

GERTIE
I don't like his feet.

ELLIOTT
They're only feet, you little twerp. (*to
Michael*) Here. (*to Gertie and Michael*) He's
trying to tell us something.

Elliott hands the globe to Michael, and opens the
atlas once again. As he rifles through the pages, E.T.
extends his hand, stopping him at a page which is a
map of the universe.

Elliott points to the globe and to the planet Earth in the drawing.

ELLIOTT
Earth. Home. Home. Home.

E.T. starts picking up the clay balls Gertie has placed on the table. He starts to roll them, then begins placing them on the solar system. The table begins to shake. Elliott shivers—one of the "cosmic" shivers that run up your spine.

ELLIOTT
What's he doing?

GERTIE
What's happening?

The balls lift off the book. They rise into the air above the children's heads and they begin to spin, to orbit, really, five of them around the one larger "sun" ball. Harvey looks in amazement at what he sees.

MICHAEL
Elliott?

The CHILDREN shock, horror, and realization on their faces.

E.T.'s Ugly Feet

Melissa did something that no one's ever done for me on a movie that I directed before or even since. She put every day's work on cards. She put the entire script of that day, not the whole week, on little three by five cards. She included the dialogue and the stage directions. These cards gave me amazing confidence.

Rather than going through the unwieldy script which is full of notes, I had these little cards and I was kind of liberated and unencumbered. I could walk around with these cards in my pocket, pull them out and say, okay, this is what I'm shooting right now. The cards somehow gave me the freedom to go to the kids and say, "We'll do these lines, but let's make it up at the same time. What would you say if this really happened to you?"

ELLIOTT
Oh no.

As they stare, the balls suddenly fall. Elliott starts. Quickly he moves in the direction of the bedroom window. Michael follows.

Harvey's ears perk up, and he looks in the direction of the window.

Elliott shivers, his face reflecting E.T.'s fear. Michael stands behind him.

MICHAEL
Elliott, what is it?

ELLIOTT
I don't know. Something scary.

We see E.T.'s hand enter to touch Elliott's shoulder. Elliott just continues to stare out the window.

EXT. BACK YARD

Elliott runs across the backyard, past swings, to brick wall.

I continued to try to get the kids to put their own lines in the movie. For example, when Gertie looks down and says, "I don't like his feet," that's Drew's line.
—STEVEN SPIELBERG

ABOVE: E.T. steps on the scale.

Elliott runs up the steps. The red gate light is on. Hears the sound of keys.

ELLIOTT stands at the gate, illuminated by the red light. He can hear the sound of keys and the steady ticking of a Geiger counter.

INT. THE CLOSET – NIGHT

CAMERA CONTINUING TO MOVE into the closet, past the barricades of toys, etc., and REVEALS E.T. sitting in his living area, looking through one of Gertie's ABC books. He looks up, and his attention is drawn to the geranium, now placed on a box beside him. E.T. stares at the flower.

THE FLOWER

Before our eyes, the flower turns on its stem. As it faces E.T., it straightens. In a burst of life, its tight buds begin to open, suddenly blooming, bursting forth in brilliant flowers. E.T. looks back at his book.

EXT. ELLIOTT'S NEIGHBORHOOD – DAY

Elliott wheels his bicycle along, walking with Michael.

MICHAEL
Did you explain school to him?

ELLIOTT
How do you explain school to higher intelligence?

MICHAEL
Maybe he's not that smart. Maybe he's

like a worker bee, who only knows how to push buttons or something.

ELLIOTT
He is, too, smart.

MICHAEL
Okay, I just hope we don't wake up on Mars or somethin', surrounded by millions of little squashy guys.

EXT. STREET CORNER – DAY

They have reached the corner bus stop. Children of all ages are grouped together on four different corners. As Elliott and Michael reach the corner, Tyler yells out.

PRETTY GIRL
Hi, Elliott.

TYLER
Hey, Elliott, where's your goblin?

MICHAEL
Shut up.

STEVE
Did he come back?

GREG
Well, did he?

ELLIOTT
Yeah, he came back. But he's not a goblin. He's a spaceman.

GREG, TYLER, & STEVE
Ooooh!

STEVE
That's an extraterrestrial.

TYLER
Where's he from? Uranus? Get it?
Your anus?

GREG
He doesn't get it, Ty.

TYLER
Get it? Your anus?

GREG
He doesn't get it.

ELLIOTT
(*to Tyler*) You're so immature.

GREG
And you're such a cintus suprimus.

ELLIOTT
Zero charisma.

GREG
Cintus suprimus.

ELLIOTT
Zero charisma!

The bus has arrived just behind them at this point, and
the older boys start to walk to it to enter, but Greg
enroute continues with his taunting of Elliott.

GREG
Cintus suprimus.

ELLIOTT
Shut up, Greg!

GREG
Cintus suprimus.

PRETTY GIRL
Hi, Elliott.

ELLIOTT
(*getting on his bike driving around the bus*)
(*he shouts*)
Zero charisma!

GREG
You wimp.

INT. BUS – DAY

Michael sits very concerned, pensive, as the bus
moves along.

INT. FRONT DOOR – DAY

Mary comes running down the steps, Gertie stands
looking up. She shoos Gertie out the door.

MARY
Let's go. Come on, get in the car. We're
gonna be late.

Gertie exits; Mary hears an odd sound coming from
upstairs. She pauses, then climbs the stairs.

INT. CLOSET – ELLIOTT'S ROOM – DAY

Mary's figure appears through the louvred, doors of
the closet. She opens the doors, looks around. E.T. is
sitting among the stuffed animals. She does not notice
it. She closes the doors again, and we see her exit.

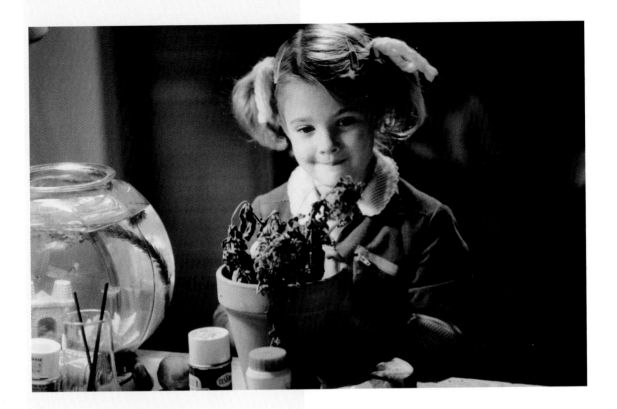

INT. SCIENCE LAB – DAY

> **TEACHER**
> Okay, boys and girls, today we will be
> doing the actual frog dissection for which
> we've been preparing, and you will find
> many similarities.

He steps back as he passes Elliott's desk and looks at
the scribbled sheet. Elliott looks on. He turns it over,
and replaces it on Elliott's desk.

Elliott looks over his shoulder at a Pretty Girl sitting in
the next row behind him, the teacher now at the front
of the room and still rambling on and on.

> **TEACHER**
> As you get into the dissection, you will
> discover that the anatomy...

INT. UPSTAIRS HALLWAY – DAY

E.T. sticks his hand out of Elliott's bedroom door, that
now bears the sign reading "DO NOT ENTER." The
house is quiet. Only Harvey is home, and he rises from
his post outside Elliott's door, moves to E.T., and starts
to kiss him.

SCRIPT NOTES

Pat Bilon was in the E.T. suit for the scene
where Harvey the dog licks E.T. Bilon was
sprayed with liquid beef to motivate the dog
but it worked a little too well. The dog got
carried away and jumped on E.T.

An early idea for this scene was that E.T.
would be made of subatomic particles that
can move through solid matters. When he
is drunk, he would, for instance, go right
through a chair. The concept proved far too
complicated and was abandoned.

INT. SCIENCE LAB – DAY

> **TEACHER**
> The scalpel is very sharp. Use discretion
> when you are cutting. There will be very
> little blood. There may be a few body fluids.

INT. KITCHEN – DAY

An empty kitchen. E.T. enters from the living room.

E.T. Eats

I made the creature a botanist vegetarian who never eats meat, only junk food, vegetables, and Coors. E.T. comes from a very wet humid planet with probably twice the gravitational pull of the earth.

—STEVEN SPIELBERG

Harvey appears next to him. As E.T. moves into the kitchen, Harvey continually walks in front of him, licking him, etc.

E.T. moves to the refrigerator, and extends his hand to open the door.

The door opens.

He posts himself in front of the opened refrigerator, examining its contents. He takes a carton of potato salad from one of the shelves and manages to get the lid off.

He brings it to his mouth and tastes it with his tongue.

Harvey intermittently barks at him. He tosses the potato salad to Harvey.

Harvey eats the potato salad.

E.T. continues looking in the refrigerator. He spots a can of beer. He takes it out and examines it, finally finds the pop-top and opens it.

He guzzles it down.

INT. SCIENCE LAB – DAY

Suddenly Elliott lets out a burp. The other students look on. The boy sitting behind him afraid that someone will think him guilty, points to Elliott. The children, including the Pretty Girl, look on. Elliott is embarrassed, but recovers quickly.

INT. KITCHEN

E.T. moves over toward the stove and bumps into a cabinet. He turns around and walks once more into a cabinet. He turns around and walks toward the table, but before he reaches it, he topples forward.

INT. CLASSROOM – DAY

Elliott is obviously drunk as he starts to slide down in his seat. Pretty soon he has reached the floor under his desk.

The Pretty Girl who has been looking at the teacher, turns to look at Elliott, as do the other children. They are amazed. One boy mutters "you jerk."

INT. PLAYROOM – DAY

E.T. pops another beer top.

INT. CLASSROOM – DAY

Elliott, with much difficulty, pulls himself back up into his seat.

INT. PLAYROOM – DAY

E.T. pours the contents down the hatch.

INT. CLASSROOM – DAY

Elliott looks at Pretty Girl.

INT. PLAYROOM – DAY

Gertie's Speak & Spell is lying on the coffee table. E.T. presses a button on the toy. The game speaks to him.

> **SPEAK & SPELL VOICE**
> X-W-V-U-A-F-P

> **MALE VOICE** (*over toy speaker*)
> That is incorrect. The correct spelling of "nuisance" is N-U-I-S-A-N-C-E.

The T.V. remote control is lying beside the Speak & Spell. E.T., holding a beer in his right hand, picks it up with his left hand and starts pressing buttons.

The T.V. comes on.

INSERT cartoon.

E.T. reacts and screams and throws a beer can at it.

BACK TO E.T.

He presses another button.

INSERT

A spaceship program comes on.

BACK TO E.T.

E.T. watches with interest.

INT. CLASSROOM – DAY

The teacher walks around room dropping cotton balls into jars with frogs in them.

> **TEACHER**
> Now, class, these are the cotton balls with the chloroform. And, as soon as I get them all in, be sure and put the lid on right away. Now, that's it. That will start them going to sleep. And they won't feel

Concept Meeting

One day all the kids go to school and E.T. is totally alone in the house. The house is his for the first time. It will be a whole sequence where he discovers things for the first time. . . . I would love to see him discovering things that the kids don't see him discover. You hear thump, bump, crash so the mother comes running out and E.T. hides and becomes one of the stuffed animals. The mother looks around and does not see him.

—STEVEN SPIELBERG, AS QUOTED FROM THE TRANSCRIPT OF A CONCEPT MEETING WITH MELISSA MATHISON, OCTOBER 28, 1980

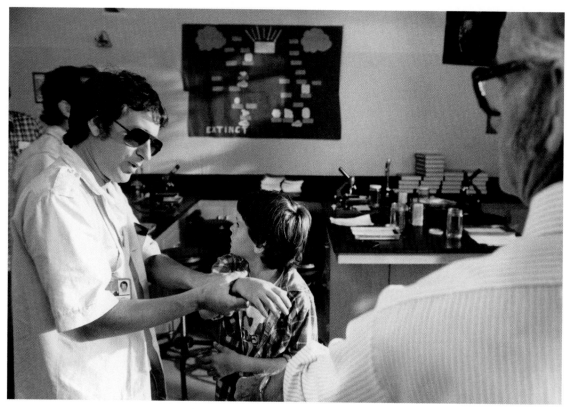

ABOVE: Steven Spielberg rehearses with Henry Thomas for the science class scene where Elliott saves the frogs from dissection.

anything. They won't be hurt. It will take a little while. If you don't want to watch them, you don't have to.

> **ELLIOTT** (*to frogs*)
> Say hi. Can you talk? Can you say hi?

INT. KITCHEN

E.T. picks himself up, looking very drunk, to the table.

He spots a newspaper cartoon beside him, and pulls it in front of him. He glances at it.

It is a Buck Rogers cartoon.

This gives him an idea. He looks toward the playroom, spotting things.

INSERT – THE TELEVISION

A telephone commercial is on the T.V. at the moment.

E.T. looks to the Speak & Spell and remote control on the coffee table.

He looks back to the cartoon.

E.T. is on his feet, holding the cartoon. He spins around, spotting items.

INT. CLASSROOM – DAY

ELLIOTT is looking into his jar sympathetically, when suddenly he has the same, clear "thought" that E.T. had.

> **ELLIOTT** (*to himself*)
> Save him.

ELLIOTT looks down at the frog, and in an instant, pulls the top from the jar, reaches in, and turns the jar upside down, freeing the frog. The Pretty Girl, next to ELLIOTT, stares at him.

> **ELLIOTT**
> Run for your life! Back to the river! Back to the forest! Run!

E.T.'s Makeup

A makeup artist was in charge of spraying E.T. to keep him looking fresh. One day, the artist told E.T. to turn his head and the operator complied, scaring the artist.

ABOVE: E.T. gets a touchup on set during filming.

The E.T. Family

The chemistry between all of us was so real that we really did feel like a family. We knew we were doing something special and important, but there wasn't any pressure and we made the experience as fun as possible. When the film came out, it seemed it was hitting people the same way it had hit all of us when we were making it. There was a perfect connection between what had happened on the set and what was happening with the audience watching the film. At the time the film came out, I had never been outside California. But when I traveled to the different countries for the foreign releases of *E.T.*, my whole perception of the world changed. I found out how big it was and how different people were. It was really cool to see my character dubbed and speaking all those different languages. But most of all, it seemed everyone was having a profound and heartfelt experience watching the film. I think *E.T.* really taught me that there are no boundaries in friendship. It opened me up as a person, and made me who I am today.

—DREW BARRYMORE

I didn't have children back in the early eighties and suddenly, on set, I was becoming a father. Every single day, I felt like I was a father to Drew, Henry, and Robert. It felt good. I think I have a big family now because it felt pretty good having three kids back then.

—STEVEN SPIELBERG

I had lived in communes for a dozen years before coming to the set of *E.T.* and the set was exactly that: a commune. There were lots of kids running around, everybody was family, everyone knew each other, and everyone was working. I loved the character I played in the film because Steven allowed him to be compassionate and sensitive. He was saying, you can still keep the best part of being a child when you grow up. The 80s were a turbulent time. And I always felt that one of the things that made people love this film was if two or three people as far apart as E.T. and those children could bridge a gap and communicate and love each other, then there was no two people on earth that were that far apart. And it just seems to me that in a time like today that's fraught with cultural misunderstandings and danger and hatred, that this message is being replayed.

—PETER COYOTE

Elliott rapidly moves to the Pretty Girl and takes her frog jar, releases the frogs, turns around to the table behind him, jumps over it, and reaching the other side, he again releases the frogs.

> **ELLIOTT**
> I want to save you! Let's get outta here!

He moves to the next table and the boy he had made faces at earlier is there, and they struggle as ELLIOTT tries to take his jar to release the frog.

> **ELLIOTT**
> Get out! I gotta let him go!

The teacher steps in, pulling ELLIOTT away.

ELLIOTT trying to break away from him, retorts.

> **ELLIOTT**
> You've gotta save him!

He pulls away and moves to another table.

INT. KITCHEN

E.T. moves back to the coffee table. He picks up the Speak & Spell, and then something on the television attracts his attention.

INSERT

T.V. cuts to soppy love scene from old movie, *The Quiet Man*.

E.T. watches engrossed.

INT. CLASSROOM – DAY

The class is in total turmoil. One girl stands transfixed in this midst, holding a frog in each hand.

ELLIOTT moves about as if in a daze. He has a thought from E.T.

The Pretty Girl is standing on a chair, as the rest of the class is on their knees trying to pick up frogs freed when the glass cage apparently overturned, which lies on the floor behind them.

SCRIPT NOTES

The movie playing on the family television is *The Quiet Man*. The same sound from the movie insert is used when Elliott kisses the girl.

INSERT

The hero grabs the heroine, pulls her head back, and kisses her.

INT. CLASSROOM – DAY

A boy is seen crawling along the floor looking for frogs. The Pretty Girl enters and starts for the exit door. Just as she arrives, ELLIOTT grabs her arm and spins her around. The boy ELLIOTT had made the faces at is crawling around on the floor and comes between ELLIOTT and Pretty Girl's feet. ELLIOTT steps up on his back, lowering him to floor, but elevating ELLIOTT up to Pretty Girl's height. ELLIOTT kisses her.

Frogs & Kissing the Girl

I remember sitting down and reading the script for the first time and thinking, "Okay, spaceship, cool. Alien, cool. Kissing a girl? No way. Do I have to do this?"
—HENRY THOMAS

As a kid, I set free about five of the frogs we were supposed to dissect in science class. I let them go and never got caught. So, what the heck, I put it in the movie.

The toughest thing Henry had to do was kiss the girl on the first day of shooting. He really did not want to do it. In the school scene he stands on top of his classmate to be tall enough to kiss the girl right smack on the lips. He did not want to do this. He didn't want to be a movie actor. At that moment, I saw him giving up his entire career.
—STEVEN SPIELBERG

RIGHT: The "Pretty Girl" Elliott kisses is Erika Eleniak, who eventually starred on Baywatch.

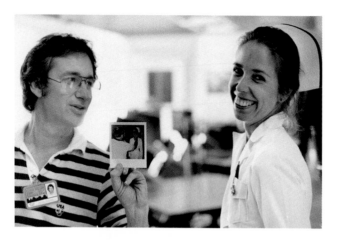

The Nurse

I had this little part in the movie where I'm a nurse. Elliott is acting so berserko in class that they send him down to the school nurse.

They dressed me in this nurse's outfit. I remember there was a big discussion about whether my hair should be flat or sticking out. They chose sticking out.

Luckily, I was only a silhouette. I didn't have to talk but I did have to grab Elliott by the arm. At one point Henry complained that I was grabbing him too hard.

Thank goodness, the scene was cut from the movie.

—MELISSA MATHISON

Suddenly two arms reach out and grab ELLIOTT by the scruff of the neck. It is the teacher. Pretty Girl looks on in a state of ecstasy, as the teacher holding ELLIOTT's arm marches him away.

EXT. CLASSROOM WINDOWS

We see children move to windows, dropping frogs out.

AREA NEAR TELEVISION

We see a blanket laden with the blender and other items, Speak & Spell, remote, etc., being pulled behind the T.V.

We hear a door opening off camera, and Harvey comes leaping out and disappears.

ANGLE ON MARY as she enters, followed by Gertie. She is loaded down with bags of groceries and dry cleaning. She cannot see E.T. standing between the playroom and the kitchen.

INT. KITCHEN – DAY

Mary puts the dry cleaning down on the table, along with her sweater, and moves to the refrigerator. Gertie has moved just before her, seeing E.T. Mary does not see him.

> GERTIE
> Here he is.

> MARY
> Here's who?

She opens the refrigerator door, knocking E.T. down.

> GERTIE
> The man from the moon, but I think
> you've killed him already.

Mary has kneeled down, putting the bags on the floor. She picks one up and starts across the room.

> MARY
> Honey, just as soon as I unload this stuff,
> okay?

TOP LEFT: Steven Spielberg and Melissa Mathison who is in costume as the school nurse. Her cameo was cut from the film. LEFT: Steven Spielberg and Henry Thomas in a scene where Elliott draws on the walls. This scene was cut from the original release.

Gertie helps E.T. up.

Gertie moves to the other side of the refrigerator, as Mary comes back, putting a carton of tomatoes away. E.T. crosses through the kitchen; Mary does not see him.

> GERTIE
> I want you to meet somebody.

> MARY
> Boy, this stuff has gone up so much in one week.

> GERTIE
> I want you to meet somebody.

> MARY
> Okay, honey, as soon as I get finished putting all this stuff away. All right?

We see E.T.'s hands pick up a coffee can from the table in the foreground as this conversation takes place. He moves across the room, entering the playroom as Mary moves to the table, not seeing him.

INT. PLAYROOM – DAY

Gertie enters the playroom. E.T. is behind the T.V. set.

> GERTIE
> B.

INT. KITCHEN – DAY

The phone rings. Mary moves to it and kicks an empty beer can. She bends to pick it up, then answers the phone.

> MARY
> What's up with this mess in here? Hello?

She moves to the table.

> MARY
> Hello? Yeah, this is she.

E.T.'s Dialogue in the Movie

p.47	Elliottt. Elliottt.	p.74	(nervously) Ready.
p.54	A	p.75	Thank you.
	B, bee.	p.76	Thank you.
	B. Good. [E.T. laughs]	p.77	Elliottt.
p.55	Home.		E.T. phone home. phone
p.56	Home.		home.
	Be good. Be good.	p.78	Yes. Come.
	Elliottt.	p.81	Ouch.
p.57	Hi.	p.82	Okay.
	Elliottt.	p.89	[E.T. groans]
	E.T.	p.90	Hi. Hey. Good. Okay. For
	E.T.		sure. No. Yes. Please.
p.58	Elliottt, stay.		Thank you. E.T. E.T.
	Hey.		Home. . .home.
p.59	Elliottt.		[E.T. whimpers]
p.60	E.T.	p.94	[E.T. hiccupping]
	E.T. phone home.	p.96	Thank you Elliottt.
p.61	For sure.	p.107	E.T. phone home. E.T.
	Music.		phone home.
p.62	E.T. phone home.	p.109	Please.
	(softly) Come.	p.120	Yes. Ready.
	More.	p.121	Be good. Thank you.
p.63	Elliottt?		Come? Ouch. I'll be right
	Music?		here. [E.T. smiles]
	Please.		
p.68	Yes, Elliottt?	*Page numbers refer to an early*	
	Yes. E.T. stay home.	*draft of the script. This list of*	
	I'll be right here.	*E.T.'s dialogue was compiled by*	
p.72	Okay.	*producer Kathleen Kennedy.*	

INT. PLAYROOM – DAY

GERTIE watches T.V.

> **GERTIE**
> Basket. Bandit. Ball. Basket. Bandit. Ball.

> **MARY** (*off*) (***into telephone***)
> What do you mean, acting strangely? He was feeling a little ill yesterday.

> **GERTIE**
> Bugs. Bananas.

INT. KITCHEN – DAY

Mary is still on the phone crossing to the table.

> **MARY**
> Intoxicated?

She picks up the beer can she set down on the table and begins to wonder.

> **GERTIE**
> Bubble. Beetle.

> **MARY**
> You sure you have the right Elliott?

INT. PLAYROOM – DAY

> **GERTIE**
> B. B. Biscuits. Banjo.

E.T. looks at Gertie. Hears the letter "B" (for many things) being repeated on television.

> **E.T.**
> B. B.

> **GERTIE**
> You said B. You said B.

> **E.T.**
> B.

> **GERTIE**
> You said B. Good!

> **E.T.**
> Good.

INT. KITCHEN – DAY

> **MARY**
> Okay, I'll be right down. Thank you.

INT. PLAYROOM – DAY

Mary entering from the kitchen.

> **MARY**
> Gertie? I have to go pick up Elliott. Will you be a good girl and stay—?

> **GERTIE**
> Mommy, he can talk!

> **MARY**
> Of course he can talk. I'll be right back in ten minutes. Stay there.

Mary runs out through the kitchen.

E.T. moves from behind the T.V., and moves to the telephone on the coffee table.

> **GERTIE**
> Phone.

> **E.T.**
> Phone?

> **GERTIE**
> Phone.

> **E.T.**
> Phone.

Gertie moves to him.

> **GERTIE**
> You wanna call somebody?

INT. STAIRWAY – HALLWAY – SECOND FLOOR – DAY

Elliott runs up the steps and starts toward his bedroom. He hears something in Gertie's room, drops his jacket and bag, and moves to Gertie's room.

> **MARY** (*off*)
> I am not paying for frogs. You get your-self a bag and go out in the woods and bag some.

> **GERTIE**
> Be good. Be good. Stay here. Stay. And don't tell anybody. No-Nobody. Be good. Be good. Hm.

THROUGH GERTIE'S DOOR – DAY

We see Gertie, wearing her full cowgirl ensemble, struggling to close the closet door.

SCRIPT NOTES

Harrison Ford appeared as the principal in some scenes here that were eventually cut from the movie.

Henry Thomas was so excited about meeting his hero from *Star Wars* that he took the day's call sheet to show his friends because he thought they would not believe him.

INT. GERTIE'S ROOM – DAY

Elliott moves into Gertie's room. Gertie looks up and he shoves her out of the way and opens the door.

INT. CLOSET – DAY

E.T. stands there, dressed up as a woman. He stands erect and speaks.

ELLIOTT
Oh, God!

E.T.
Eh-eh-eh-eh—Elliott.

ELLIOTT
What?!

E.T. (*off*)
Elliott. Elliott. El-...

Elliott is amazed.

Gertie moves to E.T.'s side.

GERTIE
I taught him how to talk. Now, he can talk now.

Elliott spots the open Speak & Spell and other paraphanelia E.T. has gathered.

GERTIE
Look what he brought up here all by himself. What's he need this stuff for?

ELLIOTT
E.T. Can you say that?

ELLIOTT
Can you say E.T.? E.T.

E.T.
E.T. E.T. E.T. Be good.

E.T. turns and moves out of the closet into Elliott's room. Gertie and Elliott follow him.

GERTIE
Be good. I taught him that, too.

ELLIOTT
You know, you should give him his dignity. This is the most ridiculous thing I've ever seen.

E.T looks back at Elliott. E.T. lifts the Buck Rogers cartoon, and shows it to Elliott.

E.T.

Phone.

Elliott takes it and looks at it.

ELLIOTT

Phone? He said "phone"? He said "phone"?

GERTIE

(*has seated herself but now rises.*)
Can't you understand English? He
said "phone."

E.T. quickly moves to the closet. He points.

E.T.

Home?

Elliott nods.

ELLIOTT

You're right. That's E.T.'s home.

E.T. swiftly moves toward the window. He
points again.

E.T.

Hm? E.T. home phone.

Harrison Ford

Very early on we made several fairly large lifts. We cut
the scene where Elliott is taken to the principal's office.
The principal was played by Harrison Ford.

—CAROL LITTLETON, EDITOR

Working with Harrison Ford was a very big deal for
me. The reason I got involved in film in the first
place was because of *Star Wars* which was fantastic to me.
E.T. came along and there was an alien and a spaceship. I
thought, well, it's not *Star Wars* but it's definitely something
to do with outer space. And Harrison Ford? Who could ask
for anything more?

—HENRY THOMAS

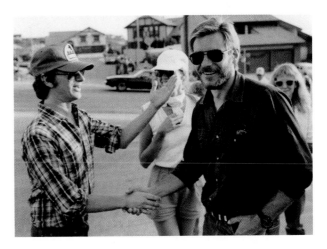

So we have Harrison Ford playing the principal, very
strict, in a tweed suit. I didn't show his face that clearly.
I just showed the back of his head and his hand tapping. I
wasn't showing adults in the movie. I think he did it because
he didn't have to really be on camera. He's lecturing Elliott
but his back is turned so he's not looking at him, Elliott is
sitting in a chair across from the principal.

E.T. meanwhile is at home trying to take all these
communicator parts and telepathically move them up the
stairs. So as E.T. is successful moving this junk heap up the
stairs to the bedroom, Elliott starts rising.

—STEVEN SPIELBERG

*LEFT: E.T. with film editor Carol Littleton. ABOVE: Steven
Spielberg and Harrison Ford on location at Elliott's house.*

Concept Meeting

I love the image of E.T. not being tall enough to look out the window of the kid's bedroom. He is yearning to look out because he's sort of a prisoner, in a way, and there's life out there. Outside are all the stars and the moon and all you see are his eyes and part of his nose and the childlike yearning to get back home. It reminds the audience that E.T. really belongs home.

—STEVEN SPIELBERG

One of my favorite images in *Heidi*, the only one I remember, is when she went to sleep in this loft. She had a little window and could see the stars. It was a tiny window and she couldn't see any land outside. She would fall asleep just staring out at the stars.

—MELISSA MATHISON, AS QUOTED FROM THE TRANSCRIPT OF A CONCEPT MEETING BETWEEN STEVEN SPIELBERG AND MELISSA MATHISON, OCTOBER 28, 1980

GERTIE
E.T. phone home.

Elliott is momentarily puzzled but quickly realizes.

ELLIOTT
E.T. phone home. E.T. phone home!

GERTIE
He wants to call somebody.

The door opens, and Michael enters. He is amused by E.T.'s attire.

MICHAEL
Wh-Wh-What's all this shit?

E.T.
E.T. phone home.

MICHAEL
Oh, my God. He's talking.

E.T.
Home.

MARY

"And then perhaps there is a rush of
nanas to the nurseries to see what is happening. But Tink is saved. 'Thank you.
Oh, thank you, thank you, thank you.
And now to rescue Wendy.'"

GERTIE

Will you read it to me again?

MARY

Okay. (reading) "Peter says...."

INT. ELLIOTT'S BEDROOM

Elliott on bed; Michael standing next to him. Both
watch E.T. through closet doors.

ELLIOTT

He's putting it together now. I told you
he was smart.

MICHAEL

I'm worried, Elliott. He could blow up
the whole house.

ELLIOTT

He knows what he's doing.

MICHAEL

Listen to how he's breathing.

INT. CLOSET

E.T. works on building the communicator.

ELLIOTT

It's going to work.

MICHAEL

What's he feeling now?

ELLIOTT

He's feeling everything.

INT. GERANIUMS WILTING

INT. BATHROOM

Elliott puts on makeup as Gertie watches.

ELLIOTT (*in mirror*)

Now, you're going as a ghost. You promised.

GERTIE

I'm only pretending I'm going as a cowgirl.

ELLIOTT

Okay, now, you know the plans by heart,
don't you?

ABOVE: *As a girl, Melissa Mathison always dressed up as a cowgirl
which accounts for why she wrote this into Gertie's character.*

105

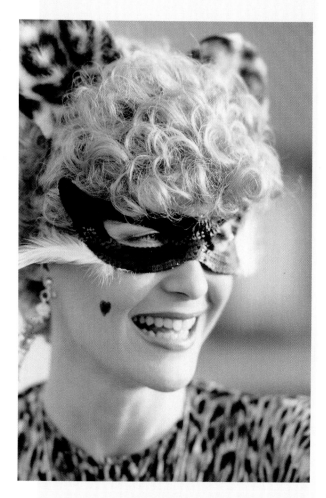

GERTIE
Meet you at the lookout. At the lookout.

MARY
(*to Michael*) Listen, buster, you won't get four blocks in this neighborhood dressed like that! Now, I mean it! You are not going as a hippie!

SCRIPT NOTES

In the movie, Mary's line, "You are not going as a terrorist!" was changed to: "Listen, Buster, you won't get four blocks in this neighborhood dressed like that!"

MICHAEL
But all the guys are!

GERTIE
I'm not stupid, you know.

INT. CLOSET – DAY

Elliott enters the closet, followed by Michael. E.T. is taken aback by Elliott's monster makeup. Michael helps E.T. put the communicator on his back.

ELLIOTT (*to E.T.*)
Ready?

E.T.
Ready.

Elliott moves to E.T. with the ghost sheet.

INT. STAIRCASE – DAY

Three sets of feet move down the steps, among them the cartoon feet E.T. is wearing.

INT. KITCHEN – HALLWAY – LIVING ROOM – DAY

Mary in costume moves through the kitchen, into the hallway, and starts toward the living room.

MICHAEL
No, wait, Mom, don't look.

MARY
Oh, okay.

She stops, turns her back, and dons her mask and ears, completing her costume. In her background, the children enter.

MICHAEL
Okay, Mom, you can look now.

Mary turns and steps into view. She is wearing her leopard dress, an eye mask, frizzed hair, and is carrying a wand with a glittering star on top. She smiles adoringly at her children and laughs.

MARY
Oh, that's great! Stay there!

Halloween

Henry would go from thinking I was his new best friend to thinking I was his school teacher. I would talk to him constantly while the camera was rolling and while Henry was in his dialogue. When Henry first saw *E.T.* at the sneak preview, I turned to him when the movie was over, and asked how he liked it. He said, "It was okay, but you've gotta cut your voice out. Your voice is all the way through the movie." As Henry saw the movie, he kept hearing my voice directing him.

He kept thinking I was his teacher so to surprise him for Halloween, I dressed up as a teacher. But not as a man teacher, I dressed up with a veil and the wig and the lipstick and I became a kind of new kind of me.

—STEVEN SPIELBERG

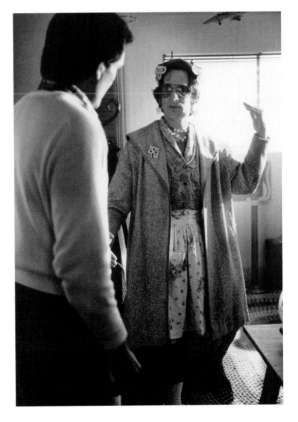

Halloween was great. He directed the whole day as an old lady.

—HENRY THOMAS

Oh, we had such a good time with Steven dressed up as this old lady and behind the camera with his high heels. It was so brilliant and he looked really great, too.

—DREW BARRYMORE

She runs into the bar and gets the Polaroid camera and moves back to the kids.

REVERSE: THE CHILDREN

Michael is a hobo, in black clothes, a false knife pierces his temple. Elliott is a hunchback, with painted face, and a heavy woolen cape over the communicator on his back. E.T. is supposedly Gertie, disguised as a ghost: white sheet and cartoon feet.

BOYS

E.T. looks up at Michael and notices the knife sticking through the boy's temple.

A white light becomes visible under E.T.'s ghost sheet, and before anyone can stop him, E.T. raises his hand and his healing finger to Michael's artificial wound. Michael seeing the finger, understands but is mortified, pushing the finger down and looking to Elliott for help.

> **E.T.**
> Ouch. Ouch.

> **MICHAEL**
> No, it's a fake knife. It's a fake.

> **E.T.**
> Ouch. Ouch.

Mary has missed all this. She kneels with her camera to snap the photo.

> **MARY**
> Okay. (*squealing*) Ohhh, you look great!

> **MICHAEL**
> Thank you.

Debra Winger

My friend Debra Winger came to the set one day when we were shooting the Halloween scene.

I loved her voice. She had a really low, husky voice and I asked her to read every single E.T. line in the script into a tape recorder. So in the rough cut on the temp track, it's mostly Debra's voice.

—STEVEN SPIELBERG

> **ELLIOTT**
> Thank you.

> **E.T.**
> Thank you.

Luckily Mary snaps the picture just as E.T. speaks so she does not hear him.

FLASH FROM POLAROID

E.T.'s legs buckle and he starts to collapse under the shock of the flash camera. Michael and Elliott grab his arms and pull him back to his feet. Mary has seen none of this; she is busy with the camera. The boys start toward the front door.

EXT. FRONT OF HOUSE – DUSK

Michael, Elliott, and E.T., accompanied by Harvey, move down the driveway in their costumes.

MARY comes out of the house and waves to them, her wand in her hand.

> **MARY**
> Be back one hour after sundown,
> no later. Bye.

E.T. turns to look back at Mary.

E.T.'s POV

He turns and continues on his way. The boys run to hold his hand, and guide him down the driveway.

> **MICHAEL**
> Gertie! Come here. Come on.

Mary goes back into the house, showing some concern.

**EXT. FIRE ROAD BELOW LOOKOUT –
TO LOOKOUT – DUSK**

Gertie stands at the lookout waiting. She angrily paces back and forth. She kicks the bike beside her.

EXT. STREETS – DUSK

As we follow Elliott, Michael, E.T., and Harvey down the street we see children, dressed as cats and clowns, etc.

ABOVE and RIGHT: Shooting Halloween as seen through the eyes of E.T. in his ghost costume.

ELLIOTT, E.T., MICHAEL, AND HARVEY move among the throng of "Trick or Treaters."

Among the throng of children, there appears a small YODA approaching them. As he passes, E.T. starts to move toward him.

E.T.
Home. Home. Home. Home. Home.
Home. Home. Home.

Elliott and Michael quickly overtake him, and they continue on their way. Yoda looks back at them, continuing on his way.

Elliott, Michael, E.T., and Harvey continue on their way into the setting sun.

MICHAEL
Be back one hour after sunset. No later.

ELLIOTT
I'll try as fast as I can, Mike. You gotta cover me.

ELLIOTT
(*indicating E.T.*) Well... come on, help me.

MICHAEL
We'll be waiting for you, Elliott. So come back, for sure.

They pick him up and start putting him in the basket of the bicycle.

Yoda

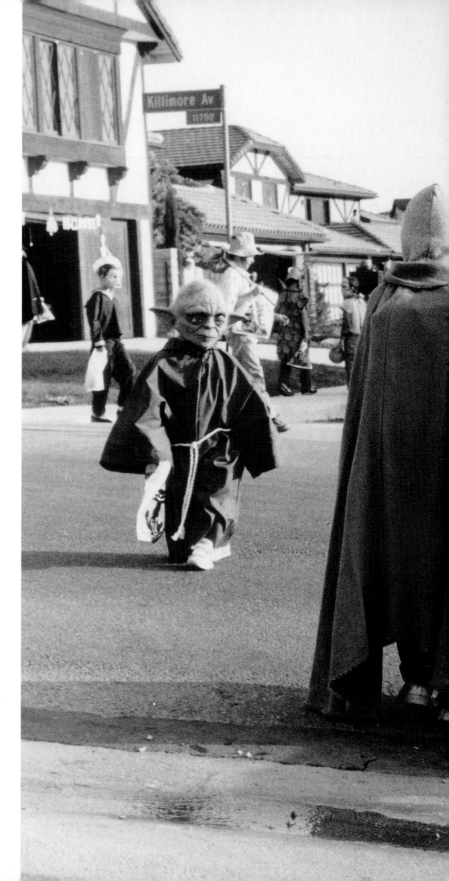

For the Halloween scene, I got a
Yoda costume and dressed someone as the character. I didn't tell
George [Lucas] I was doing this. In
the scene, E.T. is covered with a sheet
and sees Yoda coming from the other
direction. Yoda is oblivious but E.T.
recognizes Yoda because, you know,
the galaxy is a rather small place
among film makers.
—STEVEN SPIELBERG

I hadn't seen the finished movie and
when it was completed, we had a
screening for ILM which I attended.
Steven warned me there was something special in the movie for me.
    So we are watching and suddenly
Yoda showed up in the film.
Everybody in the audience cheered,
of course, because it was an ILM
screening.
    I really loved it. I was amazed
and flattered. It was a very funny
moment.
—GEORGE LUCAS

I remember George was sitting right
next to me during the screening
and when Yoda came on the screen,
George gave me a little nudge with
his arm which, I guess, was his way of
saying that was cool.
—STEVEN SPIELBERG

110

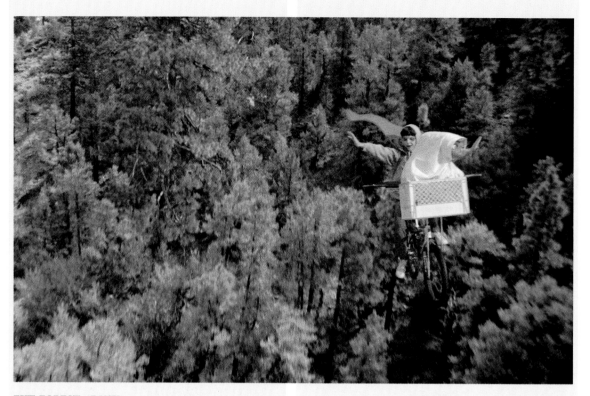

EXT. FOREST – DUSK

Elliott is on his bicycle, and E.T. is in the basket, strapped to the handlebars. Elliott guides his bike down a forest path.

EXT. MIDDLE OF THE FOREST – NIGHT

Elliott steers the bicycle toward the really heavy forest. E.T. bounces in his seat.

E.T. with a focused concentration, looks straight ahead.

> ELLIOTT
> It's too bumpy. We'll have to walk from he- e-...

He hardly has time to finish the sentence as the bicycle moves forward, and he almost loses balance, yelling.

E.T. LIFTS THE BICYCLE INTO THE AIR.

> ELLIOTT
> ...-e-ere! E.- T.!

EXT. SKY – NIGHT

The bicycle glides five feet over the tall grass and circles the landing site.

> ELLIOTT
> Not so high! Not so high!

E.T. feels Elliott's joy, and in the excitement of his own triumph, E.T. allows the ride to continue. The bicycle rises to the treetops. Elliott rides the bicycle, pedaling as hard as he can, steering through the treetops. He screams, laughing.

EXT. THE SKY – NIGHT

They begin to descend.

> ELLIOTT
> Don't crash, please.

EXT. THE LANDING SITE – NIGHT

The bicycle crashes on impact. Elliott, still laughing, is in a pile with the bicycle and E.T. His feet stick up in the air.

INT. ELLIOTT'S HOUSE/FRONT DOOR – NIGHT

Mary is sitting on the step, twirling her star-wand, obviously angry.

EXT. THE LANDING SITE – NIGHT

THE COMMUNICATOR has been set upon a rock. The lid is ajar. E.T. opens the lid and connects the hanger with many colored wires attached to it onto a disc-shaped sawblade with teeth around the outer edge.

He picks up a fork nearby which has a tong missing from it, and places it upright on the teeth of the sawblade.

There is a battery beside the record player which E.T. puts a plug into. His hands probe around the other objects, checking their positions.

He places a walkie talkie beside the record player. A Speak & Spell sits beside it.

E.T. leans the Speak & Spell near the record player, and inserts a small microphone into it. His hands check other objects. Then he pauses and folds his hands.

ELLIOTT ties a string to a tree branch. E.T. beside him directing how it should be done.

Elliott moves away from the branch, holding the string in his hand and pulls, testing it.

The wind blows, the tree limb moves, and the string pulls taut.

Over the Moon: Amblin Logo

The shot of the bicycle flying in front of the moon has become the logo for Amblin. When we discussed this shot, it seemed logical that we should shoot this with the real moon. We wanted to get as much realism as possible.

Mike McAlister, effects cameraman, had to scout locations for a place to shoot. We got all these charts out. We wanted to find the trees. I think it took about a week. In the afternoon he'd go out for three or four hours to find the right spot. I think we shot it for two nights and got two or three versions.

—DENNIS MUREN, VISUAL EFFECTS SUPERVISOR

We didn't want a sky with a sliver moon to indicate that this was a great effect shot. We wanted it to look like we'd actually shot that perfect night moon.

—KATHLEEN KENNEDY

ABOVE: The moon, used in the scene of Elliott and E.T. flying, was shot in Nicasio, Calfornia, near the ILM studios. The image became the logo for Amblin Entertainment.

EXT. ELLIOTT'S HOUSE – NIGHT

Mary, mumbling to herself, exits the house and heads for the garage. She gets in the car and backs out, holding her wand in her mouth.

> **MARY**
> —that you did this. I really can't believe you did this! I mean, I trusted you. That's the last time you order pizza. Just see who you get to pay for it. Your father's gonna hear about this one! Mexico!

EXT. CAR

Keys and men walk towards Elliott's house.

EXT. NEIGHBORHOOD – NIGHT

A pumpkin is visible with a large flame inside it. As we pull back, we reveal the craziness of teenage Halloween. The innocence of early evening has been replaced by kids in bizarre "punk" outfits roaming the streets. The street is filled with rainbow effects of smoke bombs. It is not a violent sight but one of wild abandon.

Michael holds Gertie by the hand and Harvey by the leash; they move along the scene toward us.

A house is being T.P.'d. The bizarre scene continues.

A group of teenagers are on a corner, surrounding a pumpkin. As they disperse, we see Michael with Gertie and Harvey coming toward us. Mary's car enters from their background to them. The car stops. Mary leans toward them and speaks.

INT. MARY'S CAR – NIGHT

Just as Mary is about to speak, two eggs hit her windshield and the boys run off.

> **MARY**
> Where's Elliott?

The children move to the car. They do not answer.

> **MARY**
> I'm asking you a question.

> **GERTIE**
> Anyways, why would Elliott go to the forest? Why would he do such a thing?

Mary looks to Michael. He looks worried.

> **MARY**
> Get in the car. Get in the car now.

They open the car door.

EXT. LANDING SITE – NIGHT

Elliott is holding the string. He lets go of it and opens the umbrella, which we see is lined with aluminum foil. Attached to its handle is the coffee can holding a UHF receiver.

Elliott moves beside E.T., and they wait for the wind to blow, which will start the action of the communicator.

E.T. and ELLIOTT waiting. Suddenly the wind blows leaves through the air. They look to the direction of the wind and then to the string. It goes taut.

The string pulls the fork, which pulls the sawblade, which activates the Speak & Spell, which is writing once again the strange characters.

Elliott is very excited.

LEFT: The communicator sends a message into space. RIGHT: Behind the scenes during the filming of E.T.'s attempt to rendezvous with his spaceship.

ELLIOTT

E.T., it's working! It's working!

E.T.

Oh! Home.

ELLIOTT

You did it!

E.T.

Home.

ELLIOTT

It's working!

E.T.

Home.

They both look to the sky in anticipation, hoping for some word in return.

ELLIOTT

E.T.! It's working!

INT. HALLWAY – NIGHT

A pumpkin with a lit candle inside sits on a desk top.

Suddenly a wind comes and blows out the candle; we see shadows appear across it. The lights of flashlights now become visible. One light blinds our view.

INT. GERTIE'S ROOM – NIGHT

The dolls sit at tea at a child's toy table and chairs. At the door we begin to see lights flashing across again.

CLOSER ON Raggedy Ann doll. The door opens, and we can see a flashlight pushing it open.

CLOSE ON Indian doll; our view moves to Raggedy Ann and the bookcase behind them. Lights flash across the bookcase and we see: miniwave oven, toy horses, crayons, and various dolls, etc.

INT. SECOND STORY LANDING – NIGHT

We see shadows cast on the wall in the background of the stairs. Our view moves to the hallway leading to Elliott's room. On the floor is a yellow cord coiled on the floor. It begins to move as it is pulled under the door to Elliott's room. Shadows and lights from flashlights flash across the louvred door. The end of the cord pulls taut, moving a chair back against the wall.

EXT. LANDING SITE – NIGHT

Elliott stands at the top of the slope near the landing site marked by a gate. Elliott moves down the slope. E.T. stands near the machine looking off at the sky. Elliott standing nearby begins toward him.

> ### ELLIOTT
> We have to go now, E.T. We're so late already.

E.T. just stares at the sky.

> ### ELLIOTT
> *(now in front of E.T.)*
> We have to go home now, E.T.

No response.

> ### ELLIOTT
> *(he moves beside E.T. looking in the direction of the sky too)*
> You should give 'em some time.

E.T. looks at Elliott. He is crying...he puts his hand to his chest and whispers.

> ### E.T.
> Ouch.

SCRIPT NOTES

During the filming of the scene where the neighborhood houses get covered in toilet paper, Steven Spielberg played Wagner's "Charge of Valkyrie" in the background, the same music Francis Ford Coppola used in *Apocalypse Now*. Originally cut from the 1982 release, a very small portion of the scene has been restored to the movie.

> ### ELLIOTT
> *(moves in front of him once more.)*
> You could be happy here. I could take care of you. I wouldn't let anybody hurt you. We could grow up together, E.T.

E.T. looks up at the sky. He refuses to budge. Elliott slides down beside the rock, looking up at E.T. He is crying. E.T. extends his hand and touches Elliott's face and smiles.

> ### E.T.
> Home.

Was E.T. Real?

The kids believed that E.T. was real despite seeing the technical operators, the special effects technician, and all the levers and wires. All of them believed in him.
—STEVEN SPIELBERG

There were a lot of different elements but for some reason, no matter what, E.T. was always very real to me.
—DREW BARRYMORE

It was amazing. Once everything was set to go, the cameras were rolling and you were in the scene, everything was incredibly real.
—HENRY THOMAS

EXT. LANDING SITE – DAWN

Elliott is wrapped in his woolen cape asleep.

His goblin makeup has smeared and run, and he looks terrible. Elliott wakes up with a shudder. He looks around him.

E.T. is gone. He rises and moves to the communicator and tests it.

He starts moving around and looking for E.T. He moves up the slope.

> **ELLIOTT**
> E.T.? E.T.?!

INT. KITCHEN – DAWN

Mary moves toward the refrigerator. A uniformed man stands nearby. (We never see the policeman's face)

> **POLICEMAN**
> Uh, how was he dressed when last seen?

She opens the door of the refrigerator and puts a quart of milk away. She stands looking for something in the refrigerator.

> **MARY**
> He was dressed as a...hunchback.

> **POLICEMAN**
> Hunchback.

Michael and Gertie are seated nearby.

> **POLICEMAN**
> Is there anything to indicate that he, he might have run away? Any family problems or recent arguments?

> **MARY**
> Um, my husband and I just separated recently, and...it hasn't been easy on the children. But....

Mary looks to him.

> **GERTIE**
> My father's in Mexico.

> **MARY**
> But run away? I— Where would he have gone?

Mary closes the refrigerator door, revealing Elliott standing behind it.

> **MICHAEL** (*overlapping*)
> Elliott!

> **MARY**
> Elliott.

Michael, Gertie, and Mary all run to Elliott. Mary is down on her knees hugging him.

> **MARY**
> Oh, Elliott! Don't ever do this again, Elliott! Oh, oh, my— You're so hot.

Elliott looks terrible. His makeup has run and is smeared all over his face, and he is definitely ill. His cape is around him; he is shivering.

> **MARY**
> (*to Gertie*)
> Run up and draw him a bath. Quick, Gert.
> (*Gertie goes out.*)

MARY

(*to Elliott*)
Sorry I yelled at you.

She moves him to a seat, then remembers the policeman. She rises to him.

MARY

Um...thanks very much for all your trouble.

She backs him out of the room.

Elliott looks to Michael.

ELLIOTT

Is he here?

Michael shakes his head no.

ELLIOTT

You gotta find him, Mike.

MICHAEL

Where is he?

ELLIOTT

In the forest. The bald spot. You gotta find him.

EXT. ELLIOTT'S HOUSE – DAY

Michael gets on the bicycle in the garage and goes careening down the driveway on Elliott's bicycle.

EXT. STREET – DAY

A car pulls out and follows Michael. We can see the forms of three men sitting in the car.

ANGLE FROM INSIDE THE CAR

The men follow Michael down the street. He makes a left turn.

SIDE ANGLE

We are on a suburban street as Michael comes by and the car is still following. Michael looks over his shoulder and sees the blue car.

Michael still driving along a neighborhood street, once more looks over his shoulder. He is sure he is being followed. He turns around a corner.

He is pumping the bike up a hill with the blue car still on his trail. He frantically looks about for some way out. He makes a turn into a driveway of a house.

We are in an alleyway overlooking the backyard of a house. We see Michael frantically driving around the house, across the grass, through the gate, up the alley. The blue car has found an opening into the alley. They almost meet, but Michael continues on. He must find a way out. He skids and barrels up an incline leading to

Facts and Figures: The Character of E.T.

- Steven Spielberg averaged fifteen takes on E.T. and three on the human actors.

- E.T.'s legs were sculpted by artist Lauron Marems. Steven Spielberg sent Marems to the parking lot to look at the rubber housing on his car's stick shift which was how he wanted E.T.'s legs to look.

- Construction of the creature began in March of 1981, seven months before the film began shooting.

- E.T. is forty-eight inches high with the neck at rest and fifty-six inches tall when the neck is extended. The head is twenty inches long and the eyes are three inches in diameter.

- A pair of gloves were made out of latex that were finer than surgical gloves. The gloves had zippers and tubes that allowed for the infusion of air to simulate a pulse. Caprice Rothe auditioned with six other mimes and won the part of E.T.'s hands.

- As a prop, E.T. was insured for $1,200,000.

ABOVE: Carlo Rambaldi and his staff work on E.T.

119

and quickly moves down the hill to the creek carrying E.T.'s ghost sheet in his hand.

WHAT HE SEES: Lying in the creek, his head twisted at a grotesque angle, is E.T.

> **MICHAEL**
> No! No!

BACK TO MICHAEL

Michael stoops down. The spaceman is breathing heavily. His inclination is to touch him but somehow he momentarily can't.

A HELICOPTER is heard over head. Michael looks up and immediately reacts, covering E.T. with the sheet, hiding him from view.

EXT. HOUSE – DAY

Establishing shot, then Keys enters (shadow).

INT. HALLWAY – MARY'S BEDROOM – DAY

Mary moves up the steps, and Michael moves to meet her.

a pathway. He has stopped them; they cannot climb the incline; and he continues on his way.

EXT. FIRE ROAD – DAY

Michael huffs and puffs the bicycle up the dirt road.

EXT. FOREST – DAY

Michael moves through the forest on Elliott's bike. He arrives at the slope of the landing site and descends it. He gets off his bike and moves around frantically, looking for and calling E.T.

> **MICHAEL**
> E.T.! E.T.! E.T.!

He moves to the communicator.

He looks around at E.T.'s effort, then spots something at the top of the slope. He moves toward it.

AT THE TOP OF THE SLOPE

Michael moves up the slope to find E.T.'s ghost sheet hanging on the gate there. He holds it in his hand and looks around some more.

MICHAEL moves across a bridge over a creek, his eyes everywhere.

EXT. CREEK – DAY

Michael sees something at the creek. He stops his bike,

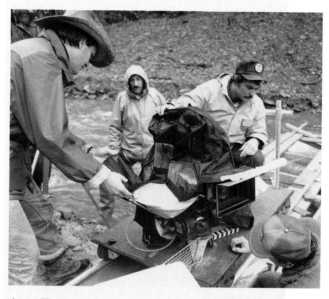

ABOVE: The crew sets up a scene where E.T. is found in the creek bed.

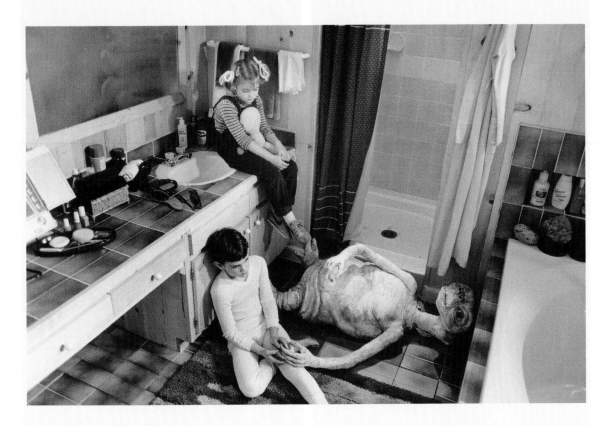

MICHAEL
Mom? Would you come with me?

MARY
What is it?

She moves up the stairs to him, and into the bedroom.

MICHAEL
Mary, just come with me.

MARY
Michael, what?

They move to the bathroom door in Mary's room.

MICHAEL
Mom, remember the goblin?

MARY
Michael, what are you talking about?

They are at the door.

MICHAEL
Just swear the most excellent promise you
can make.

MARY
Michael.

Mary impatiently looks at him. Michael musters his
courage, opens the door, and moves in beside the tub
to kneel.

INT. BATHROOM

In the bathroom, Elliott and E.T. are both on the floor,
sick. Gertie sits on top of the sink, looking sadly on.

Mary's first impression is that it is one of their toys.
She is going to go along with the joke.

MARY
That's terrific.

E.T. turns his head to her and extends his arm. The
sight for Mary is repulsive.

E.T.
Mom.

She is out of control. Her hand relaxes, spilling the coffee in the cup she is carrying to the floor.

ELLIOTT
We're sick. I think we're dying.

She speaks to Michael without taking her eyes off E.T.

MARY
Michael. Go downstairs.

Michael hesitates.

MICHAEL
Mom, it's okay.

Mary frightened, nauseated.

GERTIE
He's not gonna hurt you, Mom.

MICHAEL
He's not gonna hurt you.

MARY
(*she reaches to Michael*)
Michael, get her downstairs!

GERTIE
He's the man from the moon. The man from the moon!

Michael moves to Gertie, picks her up off the sink, and moves out of the bathroom with her.

Mary reaches in and picks Elliott up off the floor and runs out of the bathroom. Elliott weakly protests.

ELLIOTT
You don't know him! You don't know him!

E.T.
Mom!

E.T. is alone. He reaches his arms out to her.

ELLIOTT
We can't leave him alone!

Mary continues on her way, paying no heed.

INT. STAIRWAY – DAY

Michael enters carrying Gertie piggyback, and runs down steps. Mary enters, carrying Elliott in front of her. Elliott protests as Mary starts down the steps.

INT. FRONT DOOR – DAY

Michael runs down the steps with Gertie riding piggyback with him.

He opens the front door and is shocked. He moves back.

Mary comes running down steps carrying Elliott. She starts to move back, and a man dressed in a huge, cumbersome, Apollo-type space suit enters toward her.

She runs toward the hallway, and another of the similarly dressed men moves to her. She backs away.

Mary, with Elliott, runs through the kitchen followed by Michael with Gertie. They run through the playroom and toward the sliding glass leading to the back patio. Another Apollo-type enters.

She and the children all back up to the window on the other side of the room.

An Apollo–type starts to enter.

Mary screams.

> **MARY**
> This is my home!

EXT. NIGHT

A line of astronauts rises up out of the dusky street.

INT. BATHROOM – DAY

E.T. still lies on the floor, skin discolored and very sick.

AT THE DOOR

An astronaut appears. He sees E.T. E.T. reaches out to him for help.

> **E.T.**
> Home. Home.

EXT. ELLIOTT'S HOUSE – NIGHT

Establishing shot: We witness the results of an incredible metamorphosis.

The entire house has been draped in a heavy, transparent vinyl. Huge air hoses climb up over the roof, and others are being carried in. Bright lights are everywhere illuminating the house. On either side, we see huge scaffolding. The cul-de-sac has been cordoned off, and the driveway is blocked by trucks, trailers, and government cars. The eerie picture is completed by the comings and goings of men in blue jumpsuits. A huge air hose is on the front driveway and men in space suits move through this.

HEAR THE SOUND OF KEYS.

INT. TRAILER – NIGHT

Keys, seen from the waist down, pulls on a space suit. As Keys pulls on the helmet, we see his entire body, and then he exits.

EXT. TRAILER LEADING INTO HUGE AIR HOSE IN DRIVEWAY

Keys exits the trailer, and steps right into the oversized air hose and moves along inside it up to a zippered door.

INT. AIR HOSE – NIGHT

Keys has reached the zipper door (the pneumatic seal), goes through it, and enters STAGE ONE of this quarantined house — the living room.

INT. LIVING ROOM – NIGHT

Elliott's house has been invaded, by "the best and the brightest": scientists and doctors, military experts, geologists, psychologists, and biologists. All have come to probe the mystery that has lived within this house. It will become apparent that they have found, to their surprise, that their job now includes saving two lives: Elliott's and E.T.'s. Keys moves past Mary and Gertie.

Mary and Gertie sit in the disheveled room, as doctors and nurses run a battery of superficial tests on them.

Mary's panic has given way to disbelieving calm. Behind her is a video monitor recording activity in the playroom. On the monitor, we see Elliott and E.T. lying on hospital beds. Mary looks up at her questioners.

> **MARY**
> I don't know!

RIGHT: *Steven Spielberg directing the action during the scene where the government sets up shop in the family's house.*

PRODUCTION NOTES

The house that was rented for the film was wrapped in a piece of clear plastic that measured 80 x 150 feet and cost $18,000. The weather was quite warm when these scenes were shot, over 100 degrees, so the temperature under the plastic was even hotter. Also, the style of lighting was drastically changed from warm and cozy to harsh and glaring.

EMERGENCY DOCTOR #1
(*off*) (*overlapping*)
Does he sleep at night? Has it gotten any smaller?

MARY
(*who has been answering briefly with "I don't know" at this point, flares*)
I don't know! What's the matter with Elliott?

A nurse snips hair samples from their heads.

EMERGENCY DOCTOR ONE
Has it taken any food, or water?

ANOTHER DOCTOR
Has it changed at all since you first saw it?

EMERGENCY DOCTOR #2
Have you noticed any surface sweating?

MARY
No.

EMERGENCY DOCTOR #2
Has it lost any hair?

GERTIE
He never had any hair.

EMERGENCY DOCTOR #1
Are the children all right?

MARY

Yes.

Not far from them, Michael is being interrogated by a psychiatrist.

PSYCHIATRIST

Did it ever build anything, or write anything down?

MICHAEL

Uh... no.

PSYCHIATRIST

But you say it, it has the ability to manipulate its own environment?

Behind Michael and the psychiatrist, we can see Elliott and E.T. on another monitor.

MICHAEL

He's smart. He communicates through Elliott.

PSYCHIATRIST

Elliott thinks its thoughts?

MICHAEL

No, Elliott... Elliott feels his feelings.

CLOSE ON KEYS IN THE AIR SHOWER.

We see and hear the heavy stream of air purging Keys of contamination as he starts to take off his blue outfit and put on the white one necessary to enter the isolation area in the kitchen/playroom.

PRODUCTION NOTES

Remembering a visit to one of the space launches, Steven Spielberg asked Kathleen Kennedy to call NASA to inquire about obtaining space suits for this scene. NASA referred Kennedy to Space Gear, a company that makes suits for NASA promotion. The film company rented three of their suits.

The following dialogue is fast and furious, with test results being shouted from corners of the room and questions being tossed in on top of answers. Many test results will be accompanied by inserts of the appropriate machinery and readouts.

FEMALE TECH #1

We've identified his primary carrier protein by electrophoresis. It's definitely not albumin.

ELLIOTT DOCTOR

Cerebellar testing shows no deficits on F.N.F. and H.T.S. testing.

WE SEE E.T.'s and Elliott's EEG machines. The readouts are identical.

MALE TECH #1

The E.E.G. analysis shows complete coherence and synchronization of brain-wave activities between both subjects.

INT. KITCHEN/PLAYROOM – NIGHT

Keys enters from the air shower, now completely dressed in the "clean room" suit.

It might have been assumed that the visual shock of the house quarantine had reached its peak, but the look of the kitchen/playroom is terrifying. The entire area is draped in plastic, crammed full of machines, monitors, and people wearing the anonymous, masked "clean room" suits.

Keys moves from the kitchen to the playroom where Elliott and E.T. lie on gurneys inside an isolation booth.

FEMALE DOCTOR #2
Skin biopsy reveals nine millimeters of organized, cross-linked extra-cellular material.

FEMALE DOCTOR #3
We're working on his buccal scraping, hoping to get a karyotype.

MALE DOCTOR #3
That'll be with I.V. and oral contrast. If there's no response to twenty per kilo, let's move to hypertonic saline.

FEMALE DOCTOR #2
Let's try for a muscle biopsy next. I want that sent for frozen section and electron microscopy.

FEMALE DOCTOR #4
We have hetastarch available.

FEMALE DOCTOR #3
Add bilirubin, S.G.O.T., S.G.P.T., alk phos, and L.D.H. to his chemistries.

MALE DOCTOR #3
Prep five per kilo.

FEMALE DOCTOR #4
A C.V.P. line could help.

MALE DOCTOR #3
I think you'll get more information with a Swan-Ganz.

FEMALE DOCTOR #4
Fine, but let's do it under fluoroscopy.

FEMALE DOCTOR #2
And a set of cardiac enzymes. Maybe he had an M.I.

ELLIOTT
You have no right to do this.

MALE TECH #1
Oxygen saturation is 82 percent on room air.

ELLIOTT
You're scaring him!

FEMALE TECH #2
Any hemoglobin present?

MALE TECH #1
None detected. I've isolated non-nucleated cells from the blood stream.

MALE DOCTOR #4
B.P. one hundred over seventy.

ELLIOTT
You're scaring him!

MALE DOCTOR #4
Respiratory rate twelve.

DOCTOR
Good air entry but decreased tidal volume on the boy. Put him on O-two, five liters by nasal cannula, and draw a blood gas in ten minutes.

MALE DOCTOR #3
Temperature has dropped from twenty to seventeen degrees centigrade.

FEMALE DOCTOR #2
Get a hypothermia blanket and some warm lamps.

ELLIOTT
Leave him alone.

FEMALE DOCTOR #2
S-PEP shows an absence of spike in the gamma globulin range.

FEMALE DOCTOR #3
He's got a very different immune system.

ELLIOTT
Just leave him alone. I can take care of him.

ELLIOTT and E.T. lie side by side, tubed, taped, and needled. Keys is outside near where E.T. lies.

The Hospital

In the earliest scripts, E.T. and Elliott were taken to a hospital when they got sick towards the end of the film. Then Michael and his friends rescue them from there.

I remember scouting hospital after hospital but we couldn't find one we really liked that would be available to us on a scale that we needed.

—ALLEN DAVIAU

Steven flew into Los Angeles International Airport and, at the time, they were building the Bradley Terminal. They had erected a temporary pneumatic structure for international flights.

Well, Steven had this absolutely brilliant idea to re-create that kind of structure in the family house. It was psychologically so appropriate to the story to take this warm, comfortable environment where the kids are growing up and turn it into a nightmare.

—JAMES D. BISSELL, PRODUCTION DESIGNER

It made a lot of sense to me that the house would be the place the government would seal up. They would shut down the surrounding neighborhood and do their work there.

—STEVEN SPIELBERG

TOP and RIGHT: Behind the scenes during the filming of the doctors treating E.T. and Elliott.

MALE DOCTOR #5
Get a Doppler scope in here and set me up for a two-D cardiac echo.

FEMALE DOCTOR #2
Skin is cool and diaphoretic.

FEMALE DOCTOR #3
We have to consider all shock-tiologies.

MALE DOCTOR #5
No, he's not perfusing at all. He needs inotropic support. P.H. is down to seven-point-oh-three. He's got a metabolic acidosis.

MALE DOCTOR #3
It could be sepsis.

FEMALE DOCTOR #1
We've drawn two sets of blood cultures.

MALE DOCTOR #5
He needs broad-spectrum coverage. How about Amp, Gent, and Flagyl?

PRODUCTION NOTES
Many real doctors were hired for these scenes including Dr. Stein (Steven Spielberg's personal physician at the time), Rhoda Makoff whose friend jogged with casting director Mike Fenton, and Alex Lamponi whose job was to treat E.T. as a real person.

FEMALE TECH #1
Cardiac output one-point-nine liters per meter squared body surface area per minute. Ejection fraction is 20 percent.

Keys has reached the side of the isolation booth that Elliott is on. He raps on the plastic separating them three times.

KEYS
Elliott.

Elliott looks to Keys.

KEYS
I've been to the forest.

MILITARY DOCTOR
He shouldn't talk now.

KEYS
Well, he has to talk now, Major.

KEYS
Elliott, that machine, what does it do?

ELLIOTT
The communicator? Is it still working?

KEYS
It's doing something. What?

ELLIOTT
I really shouldn't tell.

ELLIOTT
He came to me. He came to me.

KEYS
Elliott, he came to me, too. I've been wishing for this since I was ten years old. I don't want him to die. What can we do that we're not already doing?

ELLIOTT
He needs to go home. He's calling his people. And I don't know where they are. He needs to go home.

KEYS
Elliott, I don't think that he was left here intentionally. But his being here is a miracle, Elliott. It's a miracle. And you did the

best that anybody could do. I'm glad he met you first.

Keys rises. Elliott looks after him. He raises up a little.

D.N.A. DOCTOR
He's got D.N.A.

FEMALE TECH #1
Incredible.

D.N.A. DOCTOR
He's got D.N.A.! He doesn't have four nucleotides, like we do. He has six.

MALE TECH #1
I've got de-synchronization of the two brain-wave activities.

MALE DOCTOR #6
What are they?

D.N.A. DOCTOR
One is inosine, and there's a pyrimidine we can't identify.

FEMALE DOCTOR #1
That's a thousand times more genetic diversity.

ELLIOTT
E.T.!

FEMALE NURSE #1
The boy's condition is stabilizing. His blood pressure is coming back up.

FEMALE DOCTOR #2
He's making proteins we've never even heard of.

FEMALE DOCTOR #3
Two hundred and sixteen codons compared to our sixty-four.

ELLIOTT
E.T.

E.T.
Elliott.

PRODUCTION NOTES

For this sequence, Kathleen Kennedy and Melissa Mathison spent time in a local L.A. hospital to research the procedures for treating a patient with E.T.'s condition. Mathison didn't like working on these scenes because they had to be so technically accurate.

EXT. STREET – DAY

The van comes down a hill and rounds a corner when the tube is freed. It falls to the ground.

The two men struggle for a moment, then rise, unhurt but angry, shaking fists after the vehicle moving on furiously.

EXT. STREET – DAY

The van comes around a bend headed toward the playground.

EXT. PLAYGROUND – DAY

There are the boys, standing in formation, straddling their bikes. Michael's and Elliott's bicycles are ready to be mounted.

The van screeches to a halt, smoke from the dried ice pouring out of it. The boys move to the van. They see Elliott and E.T. standing in the rear of the van. E.T.'s heart light is really flashing now. The boys freeze when they see who is standing next to Elliott. Elliott smiles at the boys.

> ELLIOTT
> Okay, he's a man from outer space, and we're taking him to his spaceship.

> GREG
> (dumbfounded)
> Well, can't he just beam up?

> ELLIOTT
> This is reality, Greg.

EXT. STREET – DAY

The official cars come around a bend, and all park beside the playground. Car doors open and men begin running into the park. Among them is Mary. Keys begins running.

EXT. PLAYGROUND – DAY

> AGENT #3
> Keep her back!

> MARY
> No!

> AGENT #3
> Hold her back!

Mary arrives at the van.

The van is empty.

> MARY
> No! No! No! No!

> AGENT #3
> Where are they?

> AGENT #1
> There's nobody here!

She moves off looking desperately about trying to see where they might have gone.

EXT. STREETS – DAY

Michael, Steve, Tyler, and Greg are speeding along on their bicycles. They flank Elliott's with E.T. in it. They move down the street. As they near a corner, two cars enter to block their way. They round the corner. The cars cannot follow, screeching to a halt. One man from one of the cars, gets out and pursues them on foot, as they head toward a hill.

> GREG
> Where are we going?

> ELLIOTT
> To the forest!

The boys move up the hill. A car suddenly appears, once more pursuing them, and they pedal frantically in front of the car. More cars appear out of nowhere as they near an intersection, converge, then the boys peel off in another direction.

> ELLIOTT
> Follow me!

EXT. LOT – DAY

The boys ride into a lot through which the cars cannot enter. The boys are really riding now, jumping hills, etc. Elliott is in the lead, but the boys surround him, protecting him and E.T. They are headed toward a hill.

Guns

I really regret two cuts in the movie. I regret that a gun was used as a threat to stop children on bicycles in that last shot before E.T. opens his eyes and the bikes take off. The gun was not pointing at the kid but brandished in a kind of at-ready position. Also, there was a quick cut of a gun in the cop's hand when they find the abandoned Econoline van. Dry ice is pouring out of the back of the van, and E.T. is gone.

I really regret having any guns in the movie and in the reissue the picture I'll use the miracle of CGI to remove the guns from the cops' hands. I'll simply delete the shot of the cop holding the gun right before E.T. flies.

—STEVEN SPIELBERG IN 1995

ABOVE: In this scene in the original release, the policemen held guns in their hands. In these two photos from the 2002 release, the guns were digitally deleted and replaced with walkie talkies.

We'\
Lead pur
into the (
the car a

This
    kids
    back

As the m
and jump

They co
toward a
continue
construct

They are
construc

    S
    Let'

    Oka

Tyler rea
slope.
Michael,

    Han

We find
They th
the last i

    We

Suddenl
grabbing

    Oh,

As he co

They dr

Music in the Sky

One of the experiences in my work with Steven Spielberg on *E.T.* that's most clear in my mind had to do with the end of the movie. I'm referring to the sequence that includes the bicycle chase where the boys are trying to escape from the authorities and bring E.T. back to his mothership. The sequence involved a lot of specific musical cues. An accent for each speed bump of the bicycles; a very dramatic accent for the police cars; a special lift for the bikes taking-off; sentimental music for the good-bye scene between E.T. and Elliott; and finally, when the spaceship takes off, the orchestra swells up and hits an accent when the spaceship whooshes away. So you can imagine in the space of that 15 minutes of film how many precise musical accents are needed and how each one has to be exactly in the right place. I wrote the music mathematically to configure with each of those occurrences and worked it all out.

Then when the orchestra assembled, and I had the film in front of me, I made attempt after attempt to record the music to exactly all of those arithmetic parameters. But I was never able to get a perfect recording that felt right musically and emotionally. I kept trying over and over again and finally, I said to Steven, "I don't think I can get this right. Maybe I need to do something else." And he said, "Why don't you take the movie off. Don't look at it. Forget the movie and conduct the orchestra the way you would want to conduct it in a concert so that the performance is just completely uninhibited by any considerations of mathematics and measurement." And I did that, and all of us agreed the music felt better. Then Steven re-edited slightly the last part of the film to configure with the musical performance that I felt was more powerful emotionally. And I think the result is that the end of the film has this kind of musical experience where it sweeps you away.

—JOHN WILLIAMS

144

EXT. LANDING SITE – DUSK

E.T. looking off at the sky. Elliott is behind him near the rock with the communicator. A lavender light shines on E.T. Elliott, looking at the sky, moves to E.T.'s side.

Elliott looks to E.T., his emotions are mixed. E.T. looks to Elliott; they both look back to the sky.

ANGLE – THE SPACESHIP

The spaceship descends.

ANGLE ON BOYS

ANGLE ON E.T.

                   E.T.

Home.

ANGLE ON ELLIOTT

ANGLE ON E.T.

Heart light beats as spaceship lands.

My Favorite E.T.

I always felt that E.T. had twelve hearts, and each heart belonged to one of the operators. Each one had a separate function to move his cheek, create a smile, create a blink, create a pulsing of blood through veins in the neck, etc. But they were all E.T.'s fathers, or I used to call them, E.T.'s hearts.

My favorite E.T. is the one that touches his heart, and he looks up when he sees the spaceship descending through the trees to come to get him at the end of the movie.

That was an E.T. completely operated by wires that moved armatures that stretched the latex and of the skin and gave E.T. his look of wonder. That was my favorite all–time E.T.

—STEVEN SPIELBERG

E.T. picks up the geranium he had set down, and turns toward the spaceship. He moves toward it.

E.T. moves up the ramp.

E.T. enters, and Elliott moves a little closer. Harvey comes running in and starts up the spaceship gangplank. Elliott calls to him and finally retrieves him. They both stand looking at the ship as the door closes.

Mary, Keys, and the boys look on, as do Gertie and Michael.

They all watch the spaceship.

EXT. SKY – DUSK INTO NIGHT

The spaceship lifts into the air moving into the darkening sky to become smaller and smaller until it is only a speck of white light: the first star of the evening.

THE END

Ending

There was a final scene we shot where Elliott and the boys are playing *Dungeons and Dragons* again, echoing the beginning. However, now Elliott is the ringmaster rather then the annoying little brother. He's grown. He has confidence. He's the master of his own destiny.

The camera rises, and you see that the communicator is on the roof. You can only assume that one day they'll be in touch again. It was a nice ending, but we didn't use it.

Henry was so emotional in that final scene that it was hard to go anywhere else. Ultimately, it didn't really matter whether they were going to see each other again. That was not the point anymore.

—MELISSA MATHISON

RIGHT: A big cake was only part of the celebration for the child actors at the conclusion of filming E.T.

PART THREE:
POSTPRODUCTION AND BEYOND

ILM: Industrial Light and Magic

Industrial Light and Magic began working on *E.T.* in May of 1981 under the supervision of Dennis Muren.

To create the flying bike scenes, miniatures were built of all the bikes and the boys. The bikes were fully functional, with working wheels and brakes.

The Elliott puppet was fifteen-and-one-half inches high, the smallest of all the puppets. Others were eighteen to twenty-two inches. Five different heads were built and clothes were made for the puppets.

The scenes of the kids flying on their bikes were shot in front of a blue screen with the bike attached to a special rotating head. The final shots are a combination of miniature bikes and this live action in front of a blue screen. The riders passing through beams of sunlight and darkness were optically enhanced at a later date.

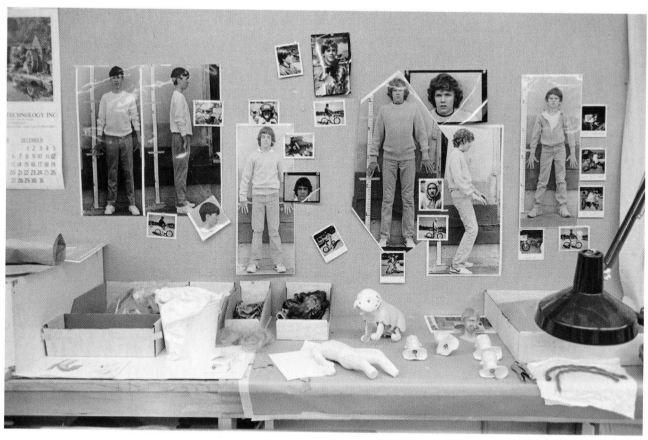

For the flying sequences, models of the bikes and each of the kids were created. BELOW RIGHT: The sequences were realized by Michael Fulmer and Tom St. Amand. OPPOSITE PAGE: The actors pose with their miniature doubles, each of which was dressed in matching costumes.

ABOVE: *Dennis Muren working on the miniature set of the San Fernando Valley used in the original release.* LEFT: *Dennis Muren (at camera) and Lorne Peterson (rear) setting up another miniature of the field landing area and painted backdrop.* OPPOSITE PAGE: *Top: Matte painting that was used to create reflections on the dome top of the miniature space ship. Below: Mike McAlister filming one of the miniature figures for the flying sequence.*

Matte Paintings and Miniatures

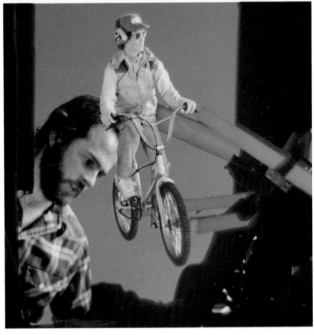

E.T. was the first film to feature a new ILM process called "Latent Image Matte Painting" which was used in the scenes of Elliott in the garden at night.

A second miniature set was created for the background when Elliott's bike lifts off the ground. The model incorporated trees, an escarpment, and a small canyon.

The largest miniature set was thirteen by fourteen feet and re-created the section of the forest where Elliott and his friends land towards the end of the movie. Real leaves from juniper trees were used on the set.

Twelve matte paintings were designed for *E.T.*

To create the scene where E.T. discovers the San Fernando Valley, a miniature E.T., only six inches high, was created and set on a miniature landscape of the valley. The background valley measured four by eight feet and was created by artist Chris Evans. Humorous details such as the McDonald's Golden Arches, neon signs for Taco Bell, KFC, and a movie marquee featuring *Star Wars* were added for realism. The E.T. puppet was created and manipulated by Tom St. Amand.

Both these pages show photos of the ILM staff at work on the miniature sets of both the forest scene and the San Fernando Valley. LEFT ABOVE: Model makers Suzanne Pastor and Jessie Boberg. LEFT BOTTOM: Dennis Muren setting up the six-inch-tall rod puppet for the field-landing scene. ABOVE: Neil Krepela, shooting the matte painting. RIGHT: Dennis Muren in a photo that demonstrates the scale of the set.

The SPACESHIP

Building the Ship

The first idea was to create a flat, saucer-shaped ship, but designer Ralph McQuarrie ultimately created a ship in the shape of a diving bell. This shape was used because, according to Spielberg, the aliens originated from an extremely moist and humid planet. The bottom of the ship was encrusted with tiny barnacles and crustaceans.

It took three months to build the ship. Everything on board moved, at the insistence of Steven Spielberg.

LEFT: This composite image was created as a possible poster for the release of the movie in 1982. ABOVE: This is a cloud tank that the model makers used for E.T. They filled the bottom of the tank with cold salt water, laid a sheet of plastic over that, and then added warm fresh water to the top. They then pulled the sheet out and the two types of water stayed separate. Tempera powder was released through the pipes, which stayed afloat in the water and created nice thick clouds. RIGHT: Steven Spielberg and Tom Smith discussing the filming of the miniature space ship.

162

Steven Spielberg also had the notion that E.T.'s world was divisible by three. Consequently, the ship was designed with three landing gears and nine light pods. The dome of the ship reflected the sky and landscape.

A number of different ships were built before the final one was approved. Two ships were built by model maker Charles Bailey. One model was two feet in diameter, fully detailed and controlled by a joy stick and computer. The second model was three feet wide and meant to be used for its shape and lights.

Building and filming the spaceship at ILM. FAR LEFT: Marty Brenneis and Mike Mackenzie. TOP LEFT: Sean Casey. CENTER LEFT: Bess Wiley and Charlie Bailey. BOTTOM LEFT: Charlie Bailey. ABOVE: The model makers created a dome out of plywood that had a forest scene painted on the interior surface. The surface of the space-ship was like a chrome mirror, so the dome of the ship reflected the matte painting. Pictured here is Selwyn Eddy, visual effects camera assistant. RIGHT: Matte painter Chris Evans is painting clouds on the inside of a bowl shaped dome. This dome was then placed in-between the stage lights and the spaceship. The light shone through the dome and reflected the clouds onto the ship.

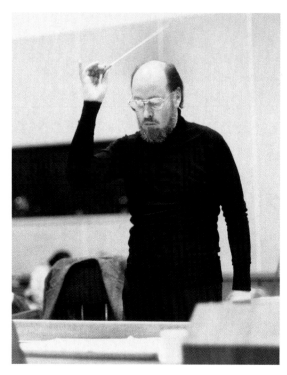

ABOVE: *John Williams, composer, at work with his orchestra.*

Music

The composer doesn't have the benefit of all the beautiful visuals and the dissolves that are added later. The first time I saw E.T., it was without the scene with the bicycle riding over the moon because that was a special effect shot added later in post-production.

We knew we had a creature that could fly. Though E.T. is not of our own species, he is part of our spiritual oneness. Going over the moon is a fantastic idea and it needed great sweep and a feeling of freedom in the music. Here we lose gravity, we're in space and the composer and the orchestra have to emphasize the feeling that we are finally free.

—JOHN WILLAMS

I've always felt that Johnny was my musical re-write artist. He'd come in, see my movie and musically re-write the whole thing. He makes it much better. He can take a moment and uplift it. He can take a tear that's just forming in your eye and make it fall.

—STEVEN SPIELBERG

Testing the Title

Five different titles were tested for the film. These included:

The Extra Terrestrial	*E.T. and Me*
Upon A Star	*The Landing* *E.T.*

The following were the results of the test, as revealed in a Universal memo entitled: "Title Treatment Test: Interest-in-Seeing Scores."

Conclusion:

1) *Extra Terrestrial* and *Upon a Star* generated the best response, followed by *The Landing* and *E.T.*

2) *E.T. and Me* had the lowest level of interest.

3) "Not one person polled defined *E.T.* as an abbreviation for extraterrestrial."

As a result of this test, Universal decided to call the movie *E.T.: The Extra-Terrestrial* which would define the abbreviation, just in case people didn't understand the meaning of E.T. Today, the abbreviation is part of our common vocabulary.

LEFT: *Photo of Drew Barrymore and E.T. used on a promotional button when the film was still called* E.T. & Me. RIGHT: *The original art used for the first-release poster. Steven Spielberg designed the campaign for* E.T. *by taking a photograph on an insert stage, positioning a young boy's hand and E.T.'s hand. The ad art later became a winner of one of* The Hollywood Reporter's *Key Art Awards.*

Sneak Preview

I took the film to my good luck theatre, the Medallion Theatre in Dallas, Texas, where I had also previewed Jaws and Close Encounters very successfully. I also had my first very bad preview of 1941 in that same theatre, but I still wanted to take E.T. to Texas. And I remember there was a terrible omen. As we got off the airplane, we walked to the baggage claim area. And a bird had gotten trapped. It kept trying to get out and somebody said, "That's a bad sign." Just when I heard that, our film came down the ramp, spooling out of the cans! And I thought, this is a bad dress rehearsal for what's about to happen tonight. This is not good. But don't believe in superstition or any of these signs, because sometimes they don't mean much.

You never know what you got until you show your movie to an audience for the first time. I didn't pretend that E.T. was anything other then a kid's movie about kids, so I didn't know what to expect.

The sneak preview of E.T. was almost a religious experience.

Everybody paid complete attention and there was a real feeling of identification. You could just slice the atmosphere. It was emotional, loving, and generous on the audience's part. It was a wonderful, tender experience that I'll never forget.

—STEVEN SPIELBERG

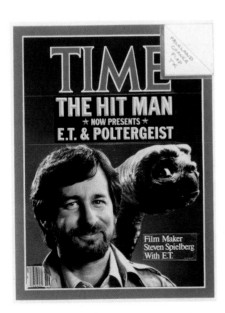

Cannes Film Festival

I remember Steven sitting next to me at the sneak preview, and he kept pounding on my leg. In fact I had black and blue marks because he kept squeezing and pounding my leg. He kept saying, "They're laughing, they're laughing. They like it, they like it."

It was overwhelming to see the reaction of all those kids. At the end of the movie, everybody stood up and clapped which is a reaction you just never see.

I think that's when we had a little hint that this might be kind of big.

—MELISSA MATHISON

We showed the movie on the last night at Cannes. About fifteen minutes before the end, people started to clap and stomp their feet. We thought, "What is this?"

At first, I thought, "Oh my god, they don't like the movie." Then we realized it was just the opposite. They loved the movie.

—KATHLEEN KENNEDY

I'd never been to the Cannes Film Festival and what a way to go for the first time!

At the end of the festival we had a standing ovation. I remember I kept standing up and sitting down but they kept clapping. I was getting embarrassed. I turned to Melissa and made her get up. Everybody around me took a bow. We were all getting up and sitting down. It was an amazing experience for all of us.

I looked down at one person who wasn't clapping. He was standing there holding up a little lighter and I could see this little flame. It was Jerry Lewis holding the lighter and smiling, a truly wonderful thing to see.

I got this telegram from [French filmmaker] François Truffaut [who starred as scientist Claude Lacombe in Close Encounters] which meant so much to me. It said, "You belong here more then me," echoing one of his lines from Close Encounters of the Third Kind. It just broke me up.

That will never be equaled.

—STEVEN SPIELBERG

Left: A mock-up of a proposed cover of Time *magazine which was redesigned due to the outbreak of the Falkland war.*

Box Office and Reviews

E. T. would have been a success if Universal had gotten their investment back. I just wanted to make the film. I had to see that picture come to fruition. So, everything else was icing on the cake.

—STEVEN SPIELBERG

Box Office

E. T. opened on June 11, 1982, and grossed $11.8 million on the first weekend. The grosses only increased in the following weeks: $12.4 million the next week, $12.8 million the third week and $13.7 million on the fourth. The original domestic release went on to gross more than $359 million. The re-release earned approximately $40 million worldwide. Internationally, *E.T.* has earned $303 million. To date, *E.T.* has grossed more than $700 million.

The following are excerpts from some of the original reviews that appeared in the press after the movie was released in March of 1982.

Watching this vibrantly comic, boundlessly touching fantasy, you feel that Spielberg has, for the first time, put his breathtaking technical skills at the service of his deepest feelings.

—MICHAEL SRAGOW, *ROLLING STONE*

A triumph almost beyond imagining.

—KENNETH TURAN, *CALIFORNIA*

A dream of a movie, a bliss-out . . .Genuinely entrancing movies are almost as rare as extra-terrestrial visitors.

—PAULINE KAEL, *NEW YORKER*

The best Disney movie Walt Disney never made.

—*VARIETY*

E. T. is as contemporary as laser beam technology but it's full of the timeless longings expressed in children's literature of all eras.

—VINCENT CANBY, *THE NEW YORK TIMES*

A fabulous masterpiece that leaves all who see it with a warm and radiant glow of optimism and joy.

—REX REED, *NEW YORK DAILY NEWS*

One of the most beautiful fantasy adventures ever made. The millions who see it will stay rooted in their seats, astonished at what movies can do.

—DAVID DENBY, *NEW YORK* MAGAZINE

A miracle movie and one that confirms Spielberg as a master storyteller of his medium. . . A perfectly poised mixture of sweet comedy and ten-speed melodrama, of death and resurrection, of a friendship so pure and powerful it seems like an idealized love.

—RICHARD CORLISS, *TIME*

1982 Awards

ACADEMY AWARD NOMINATIONS
Best Picture, Best Director, Best Original Screenplay, Best Cinematography, Best Editing

ACADEMY AWARDS WINNER
Best Sound (Robert Knudson, Robert Glass, Don Digirolamo, Gene Cantamessa)
Best Visual Effects (Carlo Rambaldi, Dennis Muren, Kenneth F. Smith)
Best Sound Effects Editing (Charles L. Campbell, Ben Burtt)
Best Original Score (John Williams)

BAFTA NOMINATIONS
Best Film, Director, Screenplay, Outstanding Newcomer (Henry Thomas, Drew Barrymore), Cinematography, Music, Film Editing, Make-Up Artist, Production Design/Art Direction, Sound and Visual Effects.
The only winner was John Williams for the Best Music.

GRAMMY AWARD—John Williams

GOLDEN GLOBE—John Williams

The E.T. PHENOMENO

E.T. Mania

After the initial success of E.T., MCA/Universal licensed more than two hundred spin-offs of the characters. E.T. appeared on lunch boxes, cereal boxes, dolls, ice cream (vanilla flavored but colored green), clothing and much more.

Reese's pieces
E.T.'s Favorite Candy

E.T. NIGHT LIGHT
-with glowing chest-

Part of the celebration of the *E.T.* phenomenon is the E.T. Adventure ride at Universal Studios theme parks. Since the opening of the first attraction in 1990, tens of millions of visitors have flown with E.T. on a starbound bike to help save him and his home planet in a thrill-filled adventure. Universal Studios theme parks are located in Hollywood, California; Orlando, Florida; and Osaka, Japan.

The RESTORATION

An E.T. For 2002

ABOVE: Eunice Kennedy Shriver and some of the athletes who participate in Special Olympics.

This is a movie that crosses over so many generations, and there's a whole new generation that's never experienced it in the theater.

I have two kids of my own now, a five-year-old and a three-year-old, and Steven Spielberg has seven children. We took all of our children to a small theater and watched the movie together. It was so incredible to watch the movie play with a room full of kids that were our own, especially because his youngest and my youngest had never seen it. It played to them with the same enthusiasm as it did to young kids twenty years ago.

So my guess is that there are a lot of parents out there with small children who remember this movie as a genuine personal experience of their childhood and now they get to share it with their own kids. I think that's quite extraordinary. There are also a number of kids who grew up seeing or knowing about this movie; they are now college age, and they are going to have a completely different experience watching this movie as adults in a movie theater. As much as we appreciate the world of videos and DVDs, certain kinds of movies simply play differently in a packed movie theater and that's what I think is going to be fun about the reissue of *E.T.*

Another reason to think about reissuing the movie was the fact that we're now sitting here with a new tool in computer graphics which meant we could go back and make some subtle adjustments to certain things we wanted to fix while, of course, maintaining what we loved about E.T. Steven made clear that he didn't want any change that would call attention to itself. He wanted the changes to really assimilate into what people remember about this movie.

In the original version, E.T. was an animatronic figure; he was not blue-screened into a shot. On the set, he was lit by real lights. He moved his head and opened his mouth on film. There was a quality about him that came across because of how he was created so that made altering him much more challenging. We were trying to stay with the E.T. that we had created and not turn him into something that would be like an animated character, for instance. The last thing we wanted to do was change

E.T. and Special Olympics

Eunice Kennedy Shriver saw in E.T. a symbol of acceptance, friendship, and hope for people who appeared different, neglected, or misunderstood...a shining light able to shatter the barriers of indifference, ignorance, and negativity and overcome enormous odds to win his freedom. This magical creature who touched so many, moved the founder of Special Olympics to write at once to producer/director Steven Spielberg about his pioneering movie. Spielberg liked the idea of making E.T. a "special friend" of Special Olympics, and in partnership with Universal Studios, pushed ahead with the E.T. promotion in a number of ways: developing a special costume so that E.T. could appear at a Special Olympics State Games, allowing a special showing of *E.T. The Extra-Terrestrial* at the 1983 Special Olympics World Winter Games in Park City, Utah, and re-releasing the movie itself. But of various efforts, none would reach the public more directly than a sixty-second television spot featuring E.T. that told an unparalleled story of a Special Olympics athlete's heroism and spirit. Now, twenty years later, the message of *E.T.* still captures the essence of Special Olympics—that differences are to be celebrated and that acceptance, understanding, and friendship can transcend barriers and surmount obstacles. This unlikely hero, E.T., with whom Mrs. Shriver and the world became enamored, spread his message of friendship and understanding—just as more than one million Special Olympics athletes in more than 150 countries change the world every day with their courage and inspiration and messages of hope and possibility.

The Joseph P. Kennedy, Jr. Foundation

1325 G STREET, N.W., SUITE 500
WASHINGTON, D.C. 20005-4709
(202) 393-1250

August 10, 1982

Dear Mr. Spielberg:

Today I saw your movie, "E.T." What an extraordinary achievement! It certainly appeals to the best in every person.

An aspect of the film was deeply moving to me. You took the little creature from outer space who is ugly, scary and physically awkward and who speaks fewer than 20 words during the 2 hour film— and made him into a marvelous hero. When he started to die, it touched nearly everyone's heart.

The creature's spirit was indomitable, unsearchable and unfathomable. And his good lived on in the young boy. You handled this transformation so beautifully. Again, what an extraordinary achievement!

Why this long letter? I head a program called Special Olympics, in which over 1 million mentally retarded children and adults participate in sports training and competition. There are Special Olympics events in every state in the U.S., and now in nearly 50 countries around the world. Since Special Olympics is patterned on the regular Olympics, we have International Games every four years. Our next International Games will take place at Louisiana State University in Baton Rouge in July 1983.

Stars of movies and TV also come to these International Games to provide entertainment, award medals, sign autographs and add to the excitement of the event. We have Opening and Closing Ceremonies just like those that take place at the regular Olympics.

My question to you is this. Would you be willing to help the Special Olympics Program by advising us on how to produce the week-long International Special Olympics Games? You were able to take the little creature from outer space and move the hearts of millions of moviegoers. Couldn't you show the world through the International Special Olympics Games that mentally retarded individuals have the same indomitable spirit? Couldn't you show that this lack of Gesture, words, lack of beauty, lack of great intellect in mentally retarded persons doesn't affect their human spirit? Isn't it the spirit of "E.T." found in all of us?

Thank you from all of the millions of families whose children will carry a light because of your help instead of wilting in the darkness because of lack of public acceptance and friendship.

Sincerely,

Eunice Kennedy Shriver

Eunice Kennedy Shriver

175

E.T., but we felt that a little bit of futzing here and there was not necessarily a bad thing.

Over the years, we just get technically better and better at recreating reality. So, it's very seductive when you're in a situation where you can improve a movie that is laden with relatively primitive effects, even though those effects were very well done in their time and lend a certain kind of charm to the experience.

I am a strong proponent of looking at the world of computer graphics as simply one more tool available to filmmakers. I don't think it is necessarily a replacement of live action movies for characters. Looking back at *Jurassic Park* and the way we constructed that, I think the believ-ability and the reality in those dinosaurs comes from the combination of both the live action and computer graphics. When you can literally put something in a real environment and have it be lit by the same components as everything else in that environment, it becomes grounded in reality. If we were to do *E.T.* again, we would probably do some combi-nation of computer graphics and an animatronics character.

The minute we decided to do the reissue, we looked at the chase scenes where the police are after the boys. For a

long time, Steven realized it would be highly unlikely that the police would be chasing a group of kids on bicycles and draw their guns. I suppose there could be an argument made that, well, it's okay because it's only a movie, but I think on many levels, Steven regretted that he had used guns in the original film. So we changed the guns to walkie talkies which was probably more realistic anyway.

We put back two scenes. One was a wonderful scene in the bathroom and the other was sort of a side scene to what's become a fairly symbolic Halloween moment in the movie. Then we went in and literally on a shot-by-shot basis looked at E.T. and identified areas of performance we thought could be slightly improved. We did quite a bit in that area although I emphasize the word "subtle" because most of it was really quite modest.

We adjusted some of the flying sequences in the movie, mainly because we now have the opportunity to add a bit more realistic behavior in the flying. It's not that we went in and changed anything about the flying sequence, per se; we just made it slightly more believable. The bicycles dip a little bit more, rather than just going in a straight line so they look more realistic.

I think *E.T.* is enormously relevant because, much like the other movies that Steven has created, here he really began exploring themes of tolerance. This is an issue that is extremely important to the world today. In its own way, the story of E.T. is about understanding and the ultimate acceptance of this alien character.

I believe *E.T.* is a movie that defines Steven Spielberg. On many levels this was a deeply personal film for him, and I think that there are aspects of *E.T.* that have informed a lot of what he's done since then. He was exploring a transition for himself of acceptance and acknowledging a lot of things that had happened in his personal life, such as his feelings of abandonment when his parents divorced. I think the way that translates to kids is that there's also a kind of child-like empowerment in the movie. Elliott represents a child that feels disconnected and abandoned and then is empowered in the process of befriending E.T. So it becomes a coming of age story where the child is able to do a very adult thing; say good-bye to someone he loves. In a sense Elliott is handing off his childhood and becoming an adult, which is something we can all look back on and identify with.

—KATHLEEN KENNEDY, PRODUCER

ABOVE: Clockwise from top left: Robert Macnaughton, Dee Wallace Stone, Kathleen Kennedy, Peter Coyote, Drew Barrymore, Steven Spielberg, Henry Thomas reunited for the twentieth anniversary of E.T.

Updating the Charm

I started at ILM twenty years ago and my very first project was to build the prototype for E.T.'s space ship. I absolutely loved the film and was very excited to be involved in the restoration, although I wondered how we should restore a film that was already perfect.

Initially, Steven Spielberg went through the entire film with us and noted each shot he wanted to change or re-do, including all the original effects. In addition, there were about 60 shots of the E.T. puppet that Steven asked us to remove digitally and replace with a computer graphics puppet so that we could hone the performance. Ultimately, it broke down into those two basic groups: the original effects and new character work.

Even though the puppet was brilliant, the technology was limited in 1982. Steven and his crew were very adept at hiding those limitations. The movie was very dark and smoky and E.T. was usually covered or you only saw his hand or his head come around the corner. It was very stylish but a lot was left to the imagination. If this film was shot today, chances are E.T. would be an all CG character. You would see him head to toe in broad daylight.

One of my personal goals on the project was to make sure that the effects were seamless and with all the charm of

the original film. I didn't want it to be obvious that we went in and added some scenes or updated some of the shots. I think we succeeded and that when people see the film, they're not going to notice our work.

—BILL GEORGE, VISUAL EFFECTS SUPERVISOR

ABOVE: Model maker Mark Siegel rebuilds the E.T. puppet from scratch for the ILM restoration of the film in 2002.

Running

In the original film, the puppet E.T. was put on tracks and driven along. It works but it looks a little odd, like he's driving a car. Our challenge was to figure out how E.T. would move quickly. He never runs in the film, he kind of shuffles. He's got these little teeny feet. So the idea of him shuffling along really fast was not going to work.

We started to analyze how his body was constructed and decided the creature he most resembled was a gorilla. He's got these very, very long arms and these very short legs. So Colin [Brady] and I developed a run that was very gorilla-like, where he actually uses his front legs to help him move along. We did a test animation that Steven saw and loved right off the bat.

—BILL GEORGE, VISUAL EFFECTS SUPERVISOR

ABOVE: The scene of E.T. running at the opening of the film was enhanced by ILM.

One of our other challenges was that we didn't want to make E.T. too smooth or fluid in his motion, which is usually an artifact of computer animation. There was a beautiful warmth in the way the original E.T. moved. Sometimes we would describe him as a baby crossed with an old man. He had the innocence of a baby but he also had this kind of jittery quality. So even though we had the opportunity to make E.T. move perfectly smooth, we decided to add these little bumps and jitters.

We also would think of him as an animal. Sometimes he was very catlike. Sometimes he was like a bunny. Other times he was like a turtle. But we found any time we moved him into the direction of a monkey, it seemed wrong, especially around his nose area. So we always had to pull it back towards this kind of turtle character, which also seemed appropriate because he had the ability to bring his head down into his body like a turtle. Quite often, we were actually mixing our computer-generated head with the puppet body and I think that actually gave the best results.

—COLIN BRADY, ANIMATION SUPERVISOR

Home Alone

The home alone sequence is when E.T. is exploring the refrigerator. E.T. is wearing a bathrobe and reaching into the refrigerator. All we replaced was the head and the neck. The hands are from the original puppet. We added additional animation to the head where he sticks his tongue into the potato salad. We tried to make his facial expression more curious.

—Bill George, Visual Effects Supervisor

Bathtub

Initially, E.T. was wearing a robe in the bathtub sequence which I think was to hide the fact that he was either operated by cables or by a little person in a costume. The first thing we asked Steven was if we could disrobe E.T. and show more of his body. It was more interesting to see how he's walking. Steven agreed.

We wanted the animation to be the best, so we ended up replacing a lot more than we originally thought we would. The only shots where you see a full body E.T. is when he's falling back into the bathtub. There's the first reveal of E.T.'s long neck that was kind of a funny shot. From the neck up, it's our computer E.T., and from the robe down, it's the original. That's the only shot where we kept the robe. The shot was simply about learning that E.T.'s neck can extend to such a length. It's a very playful sequence, so we brought his chin up a little bit, as he stretches his head and looks around in a somewhat of a playful manner. He looks back towards Elliott, and you can see he's showing off a little bit.

—Colin Brady, Animation Supervisor

LEFT: Scenes that were digitally-enhanced for the 2002 release.

Beer Drinking

When his neck is elongated he resembles an elderly person. How could we make him even more like a human? In this scene where he is drinking beer, we replaced his head with a computer animated head which provided more freedom in moving the individual cheekbones and the musculature on the face.

The original model had this beer just spilling off his stiff neck. We replaced it with computer graphic animation. In the new footage, you can actually see his Adam's apple kind of gulping as he drinks the beer. The interesting thing for me, as a visual effects editor, was how much we added to the animation.

—David Tanaka, Supervising
Visual Effects Editor

E.T. Dresses Up

A t first, I was a bit hesitant to work on the re-release of
E.T., one of my favorite films, especially as a kid. I
always thought every frame was perfect. It was almost as if
someone asked me to paint over the Mona Lisa to make it a
better painting. But here we were working with Steven
Spielberg, so I couldn't refuse.

One of the big challenges with E.T. is that he's more
than just a special effect. He's more than just a creature or
even an alien. He's not a cartoon character either. We had
to think of him as a living, breathing actor and so we
approached him much in the same way you would direct an
actor's performance. We shot a lot of video reference of
ourselves and really tried to get into his head. We focused
on the eyes quite a bit.

For example, we were really challenged in the scene
where E.T. wears the dress and the wig. Here was a classic
shot, and I remember trying to pull a direction out of
Steven. What is E.T. thinking? Is he embarrassed? Is he
angry? Is he having fun? Steven finally said, "He's insulted."

So we discussed what someone does when they're
insulted and decided he would be trying to divert attention
anywhere else in the room but towards himself. So we had
E.T.'s eyes dart around the room as he sighs. The first time
we showed it to Steven, he laughed out loud, and we knew
we nailed it.   —COLIN BRADY, ANIMATION SUPERVISOR

ABOVE: E.T. in 2002 and in 1982 (right).

Phone Home

The phone home sequence was very challenging for us. We called it the powdered donut look. E.T.'s got this white crust all over him because he has just died and been resurrected. We had to digitally recreate that effect which is not a solid surface but a lot of different layers. Also he's lying down in this bag filled with smoke. So what you see in the final shot is a combination of the old puppet up to where the zipper happens, then our CG puppet takes over. We added a lot of layering of smoke and other elements to recreate the original look.

—Bill George, Visual Effects Supervisor

Flying

Luckily, the negative from the movie and the ILM effects were archived which allowed us to use the original backgrounds for the sequence where the kids are flying on the bikes. Originally [in 1982], the decision was made to shoot the kids as puppets. I screened that footage and although the animation and the lighting were amazing, there were still a lot of technical limitations. For example, the spokes on the wheels fell through. Steven also wanted to get more dynamic movement on the bikes. For this restoration, we used new kids on full sized bikes against blue screen to replace the puppets. Steven wanted the kids to put their legs out to the side when they landed, almost like landing gear.

In reviewing the original effects of Elliott flying across the moon, I was able to pinpoint the things I wanted to change. One was Elliott's cape. He's wearing this kind of hunchback cape because it's Halloween but the cape on the puppet was static. I wanted to see that cape moving in the wind. So when we shot the effect, we used wires and put a big fan on the kid.

—BILL GEORGE, VISUAL EFFECTS SUPERVISOR

BOTH PAGES: These images are from the bluescreen shoot at ILM. For E.T. 2002, ILM opted to use actors for the kids flying on the bikes sequence. In the 1982 original, miniatures were used. BELOW: Model maker Mark Buck.

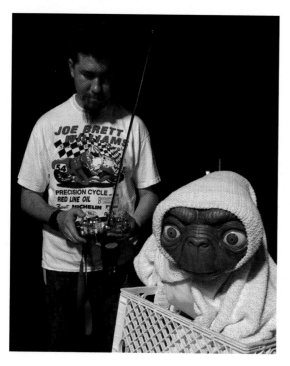

Since we're dealing with a film that was created twenty years ago, we couldn't get the original cast of boys who are all adults now. So we poured through photos of kids and had a huge casting call to find someone who could play Henry Thomas. Height and perspective and many other parts of their appearance were considered when we cast these boys for the blue screen footage.

In the flying bike scene, we have the original footage of Henry looking at his surroundings. Since we can't replace Henry Thomas, how do we enhance that? How do we make the flight more magical?

In the close-ups we literally photographed a blue screen cape to partially put behind the actor as a fresh new digital composite. Adding these tiny little nuances gives more of a subconscious feeling that this kid is actually in flight and you're riding with him. Another example of that is we actually brought in pine trees and photographed them moving against blue screen to also composite behind Henry.

—DAVID TANAKA, SUPERVISING VISUAL EFFECTS EDITOR

ABOVE: E.T.'s good-bye was revisited by the ILM crew and greatly enhanced for the new version of the film. BELOW: E.T. and Elliott in the final good-bye scene. The inset is from the 1982 release and the larger image from the 2002 re-release.

E.T.'s Healing Powers

Steven asked us to replace the shot of E.T.'s finger lighting up and touching Elliott's head. We had to paint out the old hand over Elliott's face. Now painting a refrigerator door is one thing, painting a character's face is another. It was very difficult, but Steven wanted E.T. to point with the other hand. If you look at the original, the hand is a little crumpled and awkward even though the shot worked well. But we had to change hands. In our new shot, even though we could make the hand move smoothly, we wanted the animation to be filled with many beautiful imperfections. These imperfections keep the movement from looking too sterile and computer-generated, and retain the human touch that the original puppet had. Steven also wanted us to enhance the shots where E.T. says good-bye. Here was an opportunity to really focus on emotion and, in many ways, I'm the most happy with these shots.

—COLIN BRADY, ANIMATION SUPERVISOR

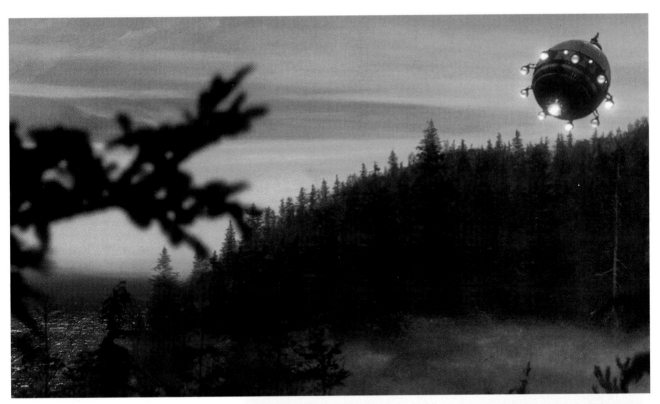

Rendez-vous

Rendez-vous is the end sequence. There is a shot at the end of the film where the boys and E.T. are waiting off to the side as the ship comes down and lands next to them. Originally, the entire background was shot as a miniature. The boys were shot against a blue screen and then composited into the shot. The miniature ship came down and landed on a miniature landscape but the problem was that the landscape didn't move. In that situation, a lot of wind would be created by the ship landing. In the updated version we re-created the landing site as a full-sized set. This time the kids (our stand-ins) were shot in the set with wind and light effects.
—BILL GEORGE, VISUAL EFFECTS SUPERVISOR

ABOVE AND RIGHT: ILM enhanced the scenes of the spaceship landing for the 2002 release.

Credits

UNIVERSAL PICTURES

E.T.™
THE EXTRA-TERRESTRIAL

DEE WALLACE
PETER COYOTE
ROBERT MACNAUGHTON
DREW BARRYMORE
and HENRY THOMAS as Elliott

MUSIC BY JOHN WILLIAMS

EDITED BY CAROL LITTLETON

PRODUCTION DESIGNER JAMES D. BISSELL

DIRECTOR OF PHOTOGRAPHY ALLEN DAVIAU

WRITTEN BY MELISSA MATHISON

PRODUCED BY
STEVEN SPIELBERG & KATHLEEN KENNEDY

DIRECTED BY STEVEN SPIELBERG

Production Supervisor . . . . .FRANK MARSHALL

Associate Producer . . . . .MELISSA MATHISON

Production Manager . . . . .WALLACE WORSLEY
First Assistant Director . . . . .KATY EMDE
Second Assistant Director . . . . .DANIEL ATTIAS

E.T. Created by .CARLO RAMBALDI

Visual Effect Supervisor . . . . .DENNIS MUREN

Casting by MIKE FENTON & JANE FEINBERG Marci Liroff

Set Decorator . . . . .JACKIE CARR
2nd Unit Director . . . . .GLENN RANDALL
DGA Trainee . . . . .JOHN FLYNN

Production Coordinator . . . . .SUE DWIGGINS
Script Supervisor . . . . .ESTHER VIVANTE
Location Services . . . . .DICK VANE
Assistant to Mr. Spielberg . . . . .JANICE POBER
Assistant to Ms. Kennedy . . . . .DENISE DURHAM
Assistant to Mr. Marshall . . . . .PATTY RUMPH
Production Associates . . . . .MICHAEL BURMEISTER
LANCE YOUNG

Production Accountant . . . . .BONNE RADFORD
Assistant Accountant .JANE GOE
Cine Guarantors II Representative . . . . . . .PATRICIA ROEDIG

Camera Operators . . . . .JOHN FLECKENSTEIN
JOHN CONNOR
First Assistant Cameraman . . . . .STEVEN SHAW
Second Assistant Cameraman . . . . .RICHARD FEE
Still Photographer . . . . .BRUCE McBROOM
Sound Mixer . . . . .GENE CANTAMESSA
Boom Man . . . . .RAUL BRUCE
Sound Technician . . . . .CHARLES PAYNE

Gaffer . . . . .JAMES PLANNETTE
Lighting Best Boy . . . . .JOSEPH CAPSHAW
Key Grip . . . . .GENE KEARNEY
Grip Best Boy . . . . .BOB MUNOZ
Dolly Grip . . . . .DONALD HARTLEY

Construction Coordinator . . . . .ERNEST DEPEW
Set Designer . . . . .WILLIAM TEEGARDEN
Production Illustrator . . . . .ED VERREAUX
Propmaker Foremen . . . . .EERO HAUTANEN
JACK JENNINGS
JOHN VILLARINO
Labor Foreman . . . . .CLARK SHINDEL
Paint Foreman . . . . .JAMES MOSS
Greensman . . . . .LESLIE BUTCHER

Credits

Set Dressing Leadwoman ....SANDRA RENFROE
Prop Master ....RUSSELL GOBLE
Assistant Propertymen ....KEN WALKER
MICHAEL DUNN

Costumer ....DEBORAH SCOTT
Assistant Costumer ....DANIEL MOORE
Hairstylist ....LOLA 'SKIP' McNALLEY
Makeup ....ROBERT SIDELL, S.M.A.

Transportation Coordinator ....EUGENE SCHWARTZ
Transportation Captain ....JOHN FEINBLATT
Location Production Vehicle ......PRODUCERS LOCATION
VEHICLE
Location Security ....LOCATION SECURITY SERVICE
Craft Service ....RAMON PAHOYO
First Aid ....PHYLLIS LEVIN
Teacher ....ADRIA LICKLIDER
Unit Publicist ....LYLA FOGGIA
Animal Talent ......DENNIS GRISCO'S ANIMAL TALENT
Harvey's Owner & Trainer ....RICHARD L. CALKINS
Extra Casting ....JUDI'S CASTING SERVICE

First Assistant Editor ....KATHLEEN KORTH
Second Assistant Editor ....BRUCE CANNON

Supervising Sound Editor ....CHARLES L. CAMPBELL
Sound Effects Editors ....DAVID A. PETTIJOHN
LOUIS L. EDEMANN
RICHARD C. FRANKLIN, JR.
SAMUEL C. CRUTCHER
Post Production Dialogue ....NORMAN B. SCHWARTZ
for lipSSync inc.
ADR Editors ....HANK SALERNO
NICHOLAS KORDA
Assistant Sound Editor ....CHUCK NEELY
Foley by ....JOHN ROESCH
JOAN ROWE
E.T.'s Voice Design ....BEN BURTT

Music Editor ....KENNETH HALL
Orchestrations ....HERBERT W. SPENCER

Re-Recording Mixers ....BUZZ KNUDSON
ROBERT GLASS
DON DIGIROLAMO

Negative Cutters ....DONAH BASSETT
DENNIS E. BROOKINS
Color Timer ....ROBERT RARING
Titles ....PACIFIC TITLE & ART STUDIO

E.T. Technical Supervisor ....STEVE TOWNSEND
Optical Effects Coordinator ....MITCHELL SUSKIN
Additional E.T. Effects ....ROBERT SHORT
Special Artistic Consultant ....CRAIG REARDON
Communicator Design ....HENRY FEINBERG
E.T. Eyes Design ....BEVERLY HOFFMAN
Medical Unit Consultants ....DAVID CARLBERG, Ph.D.
ROBERT W. SCHOLLER
Special Effects Coordinator ....DALE MARTIN
Special Effects Assistants ....GARY CRAWFORD
ANDREW MILLER
ROBERT WORTHINGTON
E.T. Movement Coordinator ....CAPRICE ROTHE
E.T. Operators ....ROBERT AVILA
EUGENE CRUM
FRANK SCHEPLER
BOB TOWNSEND
STEVE WILLIS
RICHARD ZARRO
RONALD ZARRO
Special E.T. Movement ....PAT BILON
TAMARA DE TREAUX
MATTHEW DE MERITT
TINA PALMER
NANCY MACLEAN
PAM YBARRA

Special Visual Effects Produced at INDUSTRIAL LIGHT &
MAGIC, a division of Lucasfilm, Ltd., Marin County, California

Effects Cameraman ....MIKE McALISTER
Camera Operators ....ROBERT ELSWIT
DON DOW
Camera Assistants ....PAT SWEENY
KARL HERRMANN
SELWYN EDDY III
MIKE OWENS
Optical Photography Supervisor ....KENNETH F. SMITH
Optical Printer Operator ....DAVID BERRY
Optical Line-up ....RALPH GORDON
Optical Technicians ....DUNCAN MYERS

Credits

Optical Technicians ....TIM GEIDEMAN
BOB CHRISOULIS
Go-Motion™ Figures ....TOM ST. AMAND
Model Shop Supervisor ....LORNE PETERSON
Chief Model Makers ....CHARLIE BAILEY
MIKE FULMER
Model Makers ....SCOTT MARSHALL
EASE OWYEUNG
MIKE COCHRAIN
SUZANNE PASTOR
MICHAEL STEFFE
JESSIE BOBERG
RANDY OTTENBERG
Space Ship Design ....RALPH McQUARRIE
Matte Painting Supervisor ....MICHAEL PANGRAZIO
Matte Painting Artists ....CHRIS EVANS
FRANK ORDAZ
Matte Photography ....NEIL KREPELA
Matte Photography Assistant ....CRAIG BARRON
Effects Editorial Supervisor ....CONRAD BUFF
Effects Editor ....HOWARD STEIN
General Manager, ILM ....TOM SMITH
Production Coordinators ....WARREN FRANKLIN
LAURIE VERMONT
Animation Supervisor ....SAMUEL COMSTOCK
Animators ....PEGGY TONKONOGY
GARRY WALLER
TERRY WINDELL
JACK MONGOVAN
Still Photographer ....TERRY CHOSTNER
Still Lab Technicians ....ROBERTO McGRATH
KERRY NORDQUIST
Supervising Stage Technician ..............T.E. MOEHNKE
Stage Technicians ....DAVID CHILDERS
HAROLD COLE
DICK DOVA
BOBBY FINLEY III
PATRICK FITZSIMMONS
EDWARD HIRSH
JOHN McCLEOD
THAINE MORRIS
PETER STOLZ
Production Accountant ....LAURA KAYSEN
Equipment Maintenance ....WADE CHILDRESS
MICHAEL SMITH
Electronic Systems Design ....JERRY JEFFRESS
Model Electronics ....GARY LEO

Model Electronics ....MARTY BRENNEIS
Optical Printer Engineering ....GENE WHITMAN
JOHN ELLIS

CAST

Mary ....DEE WALLACE
Elliott ....HENRY THOMAS
Keys ....PETER COYOTE
Michael ....ROBERT MACNAUGHTON
Gertie ....DREW BARRYMORE
Greg ..............................K.C. MARTEL
Steve ....SEAN FRYE
Tyler ....TOM HOWELL
Pretty Girl ....ERIKA ELENIAK
Schoolboy ....DAVID O'DELL
Science Teacher ....RICHARD SWINGLER
Policeman ....FRANK TOTH
Ultra Sound Man ....ROBERT BARTON
Van Man ....MICHAEL DARRELL
Stunts ....GLENN RANDALL
RICHARD BUTLER
BENNIE DOBBINS
TED GROSSMAN
KEITH HARVEY
FRED LERNER
BOBBY PORTER
FELIX SILLA
CHUCK WATERS
ALLAN WYATT
Medical Unit ....DAVID BERKSON, M.D.
DAVID CARLBERG, Ph.D.
MILT KOGAN, M.D.
ALEXANDER LAMPONE, M.D.
RONDA MAKOFF, M.D.
ROBERT MURPHY, M.D.
RICHARD PESAVENTO, M.D.
TOM SHERRY, M.D.
SUSAN CAMERON
WILL FOWLER, JR.
BARBARA HARTNETT
DI ANN LAMPONE
MARY STEIN
MITCHELL SUSKIN

"WILLIE" composed by Jenifer Smith
Performed by Jenifer Smith, Peter Meisner, Joe Scrima, Bob Parr

Credits

"PAPA OOM MOW MOW" Published by Beechwood Music
Performed by The Persuasions Courtesy of Elektra Records

"ACCIDENTS WILL HAPPEN" Composed by Elvis Costello
Courtesy of Plangent Visions Music Inc., © 1978

"PEOPLE WHO DIE" Composed and Performed by Jim Carroll
Courtesy of Earl McGrath Music

SESAME STREET segments
Courtesy of Children's Television Workshop

Excerpts from "PETER PAN"
Courtesy of Hospital for Sick Children London, England

Soundtrack available on MCA Records \ UMG Soundtracks

Read the Simon & Schuster Books

The Producers wish to thank the following for their contributions

AMERICAN HI-LIFT
BECKMAN INSTRUMENTS, INC.
DYNATECH LABORATORIES, INC.
EVERYTHING BICYCLES
FIELDTEC, INC.
GOULD, INC.
HERSHEY CHOCOLATE COMPANY
ILC DOVER
IVAC CORP.
THE NORTH FACE
PERKIN-ELMER, INC.
PIKER INTERNATIONAL
QUANTEL BUSINESS COMPUTERS
STANFORD LINEAR ACCELERATOR CENTER
TEXAS INSTRUMENTS INCORPORATED

Respirator Helmets courtesy of
RACAL AIRSTREAM INC., Rockville, Maryland

Lenses and Panaflex cameras by PANAVISION®

Recorded in DOLBY STEREO

20TH ANNIVERSARY EDITION

Executive in Charge of Post Production . . . . . MARTIN COHEN
Supervising Sound Editors . . . . CHARLES L. CAMPBELL
RICHARD LEGRAND JR.
Re-Recording Mixers . . . . ANDY KOYAMA
JONATHAN WALES
RICK KLINE
SHAWN MURPHY
Visual Effects Supervisor . . . . BILL GEORGE
Animation Supervisor . . . . COLIN BRADY
Director of Photography . . . . ALLEN DAVIAU
Color Timer . . . . ROBERT RARING
Post Production . . . . ERICA FRAUMAN
SVEN E.M. FAHLGREN
Post Production Associate . . . . JEFFREY CAVA
Editorial Assistants . . . . PATRICK CRANE
DANA E. GLAUBERMAN
ALEX GARCIA
Sound Editors . . . . NORVAL CRUTCHER III
GARY S. GERLICH
Dialogue/ADR Editor . . . . BOB MCNABB
Sound Assistant . . . . SAMUEL WEBB
ADR Mixer . . . . TROY PORTER
ADR Recordist . . . . LAVERNE DEWBERRY
Foley Artists . . . . JOHN ROESCH
ALYSON MOORE
Foley Mixer . . . . MARY JO LANG
Foley Recordist . . . . CAROLYN TAPP
Music Editor . . . . KEN WANNBERG
Research Consultant . . . . LAURENT BOUZEREAU

SPECIAL VISUAL EFFECTS AND ANIMATION by
INDUSTRIAL LIGHT & MAGIC
A Division of Lucas Digital Ltd.
Marin County, California

ILM Visual Effects Producer . . . . SANDRA L. SCOTT
CG Supervisor . . . . PATRICK T. MYERS
Compositing Supervisor . . . . JEFF DORAN
Digital Color Timing Supervisor . . . . KENNETH SMITH
Add'l. VFX Supervision . . . . TIM ALEXANDER
Sequence Producer . . . . JEFF OLSON
Directors of Photography . . . . PATRICK SWEENEY
MARTY ROSENBERG
Animators . . . . RUDI BLOSS
ANDREW DOUCETTE

Credits

Animators . . . . .MIGUEL FUERTES	Lead Sabre CG Artist . . . . .CAITLIN CONTENT
WAYNE GILBERT	Sabre CG Artists . . . . .MARK CASEY
SHAWN KELLY	CATHERINE TATE
GREGORY KYLE	Rebel Unit Artist . . . . .BILLY BROOKS
KEVIN MARTEL	Digital Matte Artist . . . . .RONN BROWN
CHRISTOPHER MINOS	3D Matchmove Lead . . . . .DANI MORROW
GLEN MCINTOSH	3D Matchmovers . . . . .JODIE MAIER
MAGALI RIGAUDIAS	DAVID MANOS MORRIS
TRISH SCHUTZ-KRAUSE	DAVID WASHBURN
DAVID SIDLEY	JOHN WHISNANT
SHARONNE SOLK	Lead Digital Paint Artist . . . . .MIKE VAN EPS
JAN VAN BUYTEN	Digital Paint/Rotoscope Artists . . . . .TRANG BACH
JAMY WHELESS	JOANNE HAFNER
Development CG Artists . . . . .JEROEN LAPRE	ELSA RODRIGUEZ
RYAN COOK	DAVID SULLIVAN
Computer Graphics Artists . . . . .VINCE DE QUATTRO	ERIN WEST
RYAN GALLOWAY	Model Makers . . . . .MARK BUCK
MICHAEL HALSTED	JON FOREMAN
ANDREW HARDAWAY	1st Assistant Camera . . . . .RICHARD MCKAY
CHRISTINA HILLS	ROBERT HILL
SAMSON KAO	Stage Technicians . . . . .DENNIS BECKER
RUSSELL KOONCE	JOSEPH FULMER
JENNIFER MCKNEW	MICHAEL OLAGUE
PATRICK NEARY,	Greensman . . . . .GEOFFREY LAKE
JENNIFER NONA	Video Assist . . . . .CLARK HIGGINS
MARY PAYNE	VFX Prod. Coordinators . . . . .CAMILLE EDEN
KIMBERLY ROSS	LISA TODD
DAMIAN STEEL	VFX Production Assistants . . . . .MEI-MING CASINO
ERIC VOEGELS	KINGSTON COLE
ANDY WANG	Visual Effects Editors . . . . .DAVID TANAKA
Lead Digital Compositor . . . . .BARBARA BRENNAN	GREG HYMAN
Digital Compositors . . . . .JULIE ADRIANSON	VFX Assistant Editor . . . . .LARS JENSVOLD
AL BAILEY	Scanning Operator . . . . .MIKE ELLIS
STELLA BOGH	Negative Lineup . . . . .JAMES LIM
JAY COOPER	Digital Plate Restoration . . . . .MARIA GOODALE
BILL GILMAN	MICHELE GRAY
JIM HAGEDORN	SAM STEWART
SEAN MACKENZIE	ALAN TRAVIS
GREG MALONEY	Technical Support . . . . .NATALEE DJOKOVIC
TIA MARSHALL	DHYANA BRUMMEL
MARCEL MARTINEZ	
PATRICK TUBACH	Visual Effects Coordinator . . . . .MARK RUSSELL
Digital Modeler . . . . .STEPHEN APLIN	
Lead Viewpaint Artist .JEAN BOLTE	Additional Voices . . . . .JUNE CHRISTOPHER
Viewpaint Artist . . . . .DEREK GILLINGHAM	ERIN DONOVAN
Creature Developer . . . . .LENNY LEE	ART KIMBRO

Additional Voices . . . . .LUISA LESCHIN
JONATHAN NICHOLS
CLAY THOMAS SAVAGE
Bike Flight Doubles . . . . .BENJAMIN DUNN
ERIC STIEF
JOHN DENTONI, III
LUKE BAILEY
RYAN CARNEY

Negative Cutter . . . . .GARY BURRITT
End Titles . . . . .PACIFIC TITLE

SOUNDTRACK ON MCA RECORDS/UMG SOUNDTRACKS

Color by Technicolor KODAK Motion Picture Film

Acknowledgments

The publisher and the editors wish to thank:

Steven Spielberg, Kathleen Kennedy, and the cast
and crew of *E.T.: The Extra-Terrestrial* interviewed in
this book.

And:
Colleen A. Benn
Cindy Chang
Martin Cohen
Shannon Diffner
Eddie Egan
Bette Einbinder
Elizabeth Gelfand
Brad Globe
Industrial Light + Magic
Stephen Kenneally
Marvin Levy
Kristie Macosko
Kay McCauley
Randy Nellis
David O'Connor
Susan Ray
Barbara Ritchie
Jeff Sakson
Kristin Stark
Universal Studios

Permissions

About the Filmmakers

STEVEN SPIELBERG has directed, produced, or executive-produced seven of the 25 top-grossing films of all time (worldwide), including *Jurassic Park* and *E.T. the Extra-Terrestrial*. In addition, he directed and produced the multiple award-winning motion pictures *Schindler's List* and *Saving Private Ryan*. Spielberg has also been recognized with Academy Award® nominations for Best Director for *E.T. the Extra-Terrestrial*, *Raiders of the Lost Ark*, and *Close Encounters of the Third Kind*.

Producer KATHLEEN KENNEDY has a record of achievement that makes her one of the most successful executives in the film industry today. Among her credits are three of the highest grossing films in motion picture history: *E.T. the Extra-Terrestrial*, *Jurassic Park*, and *The Sixth Sense*, which she produced with Steven Spielberg, Gerald R. Molen, and Frank Marshall, respectively.

MELISSA MATHISON also wrote screenplays of *Kundun*, *The Indian in the Cupboard*, and *The Black Stallion*. For *E.T.*, Mathison won nominations for Best Screenplay from the Academy of Motion Picture Arts and Sciences, the British Academy of Film & Television Arts, and the Golden Globes. Mathison won a Writers Guild of America Screen Award for *E.T.* in the category of Best Drama Written Directly for the Screen.

About the Bookmakers

Interviewer LAURENT BOUZEREAU has written, directed, and produced over 60 documentaries on "the making of" some of America's top classic movies, in collaboration with some of the most acclaimed filmmakers, including Steven Spielberg, Brian De Palma, George Lucas, Martin Scorsese, Clint Eastwood, Mel Brooks, Lawrence Kasdan, and Peter Bogdanovich. He is also the author of six popular books on American cinema.

Editor LINDA SUNSHINE and designer TIMOTHY SHANER have collaborated on many book projects, including the Newmarket Press editions of *Saving Private Ryan: The Men, The Mission, The Movie*; *Crouching Tiger, Hidden Dragon*; *Cabaret: The Illustrated Book and Lyrics*; *Stuart Little: The Art, the Artists, and the Story Behind the Amazing Movie*; and *Titus: The Illustrated Screenplay*.